JUGGLING THE ISSUES

Living with Asperger's Syndrome

Matthew Kenslow

RIVER BIRCH PRESS
Daphne, Alabama

Juggling the Issues: Living with Asperger's Syndrome
by Matthew Kenslow

All Scripture is taken from the King James Version of the Bible in public domain.

ISBN 978-1-951561-32-1 (Print)
ISBN 978-1-951561-33-8 (E-book)
For Worldwide Distribution
Printed in the U.S.A.

River Birch Press
P.O. Box 868
Daphne, AL 36526

Table of Contents

Preface

I was diagnosed with Asperger's syndrome, which is within the autistic spectrum, when I was about six years old and with a speech delay when I was about three. People who have autism are not very different than anybody else. The only difference is simply in how our minds work. I am neither shy nor ashamed about it, and I am very open to discuss it.

Let us get one technicality straightened out. As of 2013, under DSM-5, "Asperger's syndrome" is no longer a diagnosis. The now-former diagnosis, along with a few others, are collectively under one diagnosis, called "Autism Spectrum Disorder." Thus, I do have (and always had) autism, but colloquially nowadays, I have Asperger's syndrome. I was given that official diagnosis circa 2001 under DSM-IV.

Over the years, I have observed how I share its common symptoms, such as lacking social and conversational skills, and having poor eye contact with others. Simple tasks take longer for me to do, such as homework, reading, and organizing thoughts. Contrastingly, some of us with Asperger's can expand on both learning and skills beyond what is taught in the classroom. I personally do not have a photographic memory, but it is easier for me to remember things (especially mathematics, history, and science), from the books of the Bible to the elements of the Periodic Table. We find patterns in things, and that is the key. I retain the memory of a myriad of events that have happened in my life—the good and the not-so-good. In essence, the oxymoron of my life is the following: what is difficult for me can be a piece of cake for most others, but what is challenging for most others can be two-plus-two for me.

I have been playing keyboard and piano since I was eight and started juggling when I was about ten. I do not know where I would be if I had not started practicing either of them.

My main message that I tell hundreds of people is that I have not given up on my goals. I persevere on my aspirations. If I can do that, certainly everybody else can too. What I want to do in life is to help people. I want to be an encourager, especially to children.

Juggling the Issues: Living with Asperger's Syndrome is a conglomeration of short stories put together and can be read in any order. Within these pages, I describe several issues that we, who have autism and Asperger's, face each day. (Again, not everybody is the same. Some of us may deal with the same issues differently, while others may have different issues.) Furthermore, I have added several positive aspects of Asperger's as well.

I reference feelings and emotions that almost everyone can relate to, even though we characteristically take certain things differently. Having Asperger's is like having an enhancer plugged into an outlet in our brains. Asperger's is an accelerator, amplifying the perceptions that we have on the world and the ambiance around us. Like going to the store and buying a device to plug in or install on something in order to make it run faster, Asperger's will deepen everything's significance, causing us to take things to a more intense level. Those of us with Asperger's need to take our time on certain things, which causes us difficulty in accomplishing simple tasks. We learn to diligently persevere and be more prudent and careful.

Juggling the Issues: Living with Asperger's Syndrome is an anthology explaining these topics through the eyes of someone with Asperger's. This is more than a researcher giving an outline of what we face and what we can do. Instead, this is one of those books told by a person who has Asperger's and has dealt with certain difficulties in order to experience achievements over the past twenty years. I have personally overcome and am still overcoming a lot of the trials that come with having Asperger's. Sharing about Asperger's from a firsthand perspective, I have incorporated personal experiences as real-life examples based on actual events to the best of my memory.

Throughout this book, I incorporated several passages from the Bible and discussed my Christian faith. These are quotes that I live by and hide in my heart. I take comfort in the Scriptures. I apply these quotes in my life just like other people apply other quotes for their lives. I respect that. This book does not necessarily impose the Christian faith and leaves the door open for each individual reader. The sole purpose of this book is to help the reader understand who we, the people of Autism Spectrum Disorder, are. Again, all the stories I tell are to provide examples of how I never allowed autism to have the prerogative to slow me down!

I am also not in competition with anybody. I would recommend anybody else's book or video on the subject. I do not believe this book alone will end all discrimination we face, but I believe that if we all put aside our differences and work together, then that is what will make this world become a much better place.

I sincerely hope that every reader will gain insight about how those of us with Asperger's live and understand some of the issues that we juggle with on a daily basis.

> *Being confident of this very thing, that he which hath begun a good work in you will perform it until the day of Jesus Christ* (Philippians 1:6).

1

Royal Rangers

I chose to have Royal Rangers be one of the first short stories because the subject appears a lot throughout this anthology. I have placed Royal Rangers as my third topmost important blessing in my life, following church and family.

The Royal Rangers program, quite similar to the Boy Scouts of America, is headquartered in Missouri. Founded by Rev. Johnnie Barnes and established in 1962, it is a worldwide, faith-based, mentoring program for boys from five to seventeen. As of 2017, it is located in just under a hundred countries and growing. The boys go on camping trips and learn how to utilize the resources that God has given them for shelter and survival. It teaches them how to become leaders in their communities and country as they go out into the community to do service projects. Most importantly, its purpose is to impart God's Word to *future men* and train them to become servant leaders, which is what essentially sets them apart from the Boys Scouts.

Royal Rangers is a merit-driven program, imbued with adventure and passion. There are over a few hundred merit badges for almost anything imaginable. Each boy is taken on the journey of a lifetime, some to achieve the highest honor: the Gold Medal of Achievement (GMA). The GMA is equivalent to the Eagle Scout Award, proving years of dedication, endurance, passion, service, and leadership. The medal is great to put on job and college applications, and the military of the United States will instantly give an extra stripe to whoever earned the GMA.

To obtain the GMA is *not* easy but is sure rewarding in the end. To list a few requirements, there are Bible merits, skills merits, leadership merits, and electives. Typically, after earning a specific number of badges, the boys are given a large advancement patch. After a certain number of the advancement patches and a couple of additional requirements are earned, the boy is given a medal. Three of the four divisions have three medals. Nowadays, after six medals, the boy is rightfully awarded the GMA in a formal ceremony, which cannot be achieved in just a year or two. Just an approximation based on the statistics, 0.4% of all the couple of million Royal Rangers in our history have earned this medal, which is roughly one in two hundred and fifty boys.

Without Royal Rangers, I *guarantee* that I do not know where I would be in life. Since I only had a grandfather as a father figure, it was beneficial for me to be in such a welcoming atmosphere. I had numerous, amicable commanders who had taken me under their wing and helped me out as I grew to become the man and leader that I am today.

It is an exciting, suspenseful story of how I got involved in the first place. My mother grew up in the Assemblies of God in Home Gardens, California. After my maternal grandmother met her future husband, they moved to Lomita (this was not her first husband). There, roughly around 1979 or 1980, my mother started attending a nearby Assemblies of God church. She was the only person in the household who attended church regularly and usually had to walk a couple of blocks to go. At this church, she heard of the Royal Rangers (for the boys) and the Missionettes (for the girls).

Roughly twenty years later, while living in Costa Mesa, my mother was talking to a friend about the Royal Rangers, and the friend offered to search for a nearby outpost for me. The one that she found was Outpost #33 at Newport Mesa Church, a part of the Orange section of the Shoreline division in the Southern California district of the Southwest Region.

And *that* is how I got my start in Royal Rangers.

In late 2000, when I was five, I entered the Royal Rangers program, starting with Straight Arrows. My patrol was the Navajo. It was one of the most fun ninety minutes of my week—Wednesday evening from 7:00-8:30. I vividly remember being there as if it were last night. It was through Straight Arrows that I memorized Scripture verses such as John 3:16. We earned beads, colored feathers, and achievement pins. After two years of Straight Arrows came one year of Buckaroos.

To commence every single Royal Rangers meeting and every single event, we always pledged to the American flag, the Christian flag, and the Royal Rangers flag. Our motto is READY, for a Royal Ranger is ready for *anything*. We live by the Golden Rule (Matthew 7:12), as well as the eight blue points of the Ranger Code: Alert, Clean, Honest, Courageous, Loyal, Courteous, Obedient, and Spiritual.

The first campout that I ever went on took place in June of 2003. It was at Pinecrest, which is in Twin Peaks, California, in the San Bernardino mountain ranges west of Big Bear. I later returned in June 2005. Both camps evoke fun memories to this day. I remember enjoying nature, the forestry and scenery, the skits, the swimming, the hikes, the fishing, and much more.

Right after Buckaroos in 2003, our outpost changed. The National Royal Rangers in Missouri completely amended the program. In September of 2003, I began my first of three years in Discovery Rangers (3rd to 5th grade), which used to be called

Pioneers. The Straight Arrows and Buckaroos combined together into one division and were called Ranger Kids (K-2nd).

In both Discovery Rangers and later Adventure Rangers (6th to 8th grade), I grew more in my heart, mind, spirit, and walk with God. The first knot that I ever learned in Royal Rangers was the square knot. Today, I am my outpost's expert at knots, meaning that I am the commander who is always called upon to go around and teach rope craft whenever needed.

By fifth grade, I persevered and earned a few merits on my own, such as Art and Chess. It became my all-time zeal. In the three years of Discovery Rangers, for example, there are fifteen advancement patches; each advancement patch is a rank that is earned after a certain amount of merit badges. The fifth, tenth, and fifteenth advancement patches are patches toward a medal that we receive. The three medals are called Gold Falcon, Gold Hawk, and Gold Eagle, respectively. In order to achieve the higher medals, a boy has to work outside weekly meetings.

Today, as I encourage boys to work on merits outside of Royal Rangers, I use this true-story analogy: "If I had a quarter for every hour that I spent working on merits *outside* of Royal Rangers, then I would be a very, *very* wealthy man right now. Of course, no one had to pay me to work on them. I loved doing it."

During the Council of Achievement in June 2006, I saw a fellow Discovery Ranger who had tons of merit and advancement patches. He was at a much higher rank than me. That night, he was given the eleventh rank out of fifteen. Just seeing him with the awards vest on (the uniform) further inspired and encouraged me to work harder than I had been, all the while doing the best I could.

After memorizing several things, I was rewarded with the official Adventure Rangers workbook in the summer of 2006, right before entering Adventure Rangers. For years, I worked on merits solo and got them approved by my commanders, such as Bible merits, Nature Study, and Carpentry. Later on in the fall, I earned Christian Service and Puppeteer, mostly on my own too.

In middle school, I shot BB guns for the first time, worked with leather, and participated in a plethora of unforgettable projects. In June 2009, I was formally awarded the Bronze Medal of Achievement (this former medal used to be the third highest award in the entire program).

In high school, it was time to be promoted to Expedition Rangers, the final division. However, our outpost was not able to have a separate program, so it was combined with Adventure Rangers. I was deprived of all the things that came with Expedition Rangers, but I do not regret it since, at that time, I had not yet earned the Gold Medal of Achievement.

Time went on. I attended Royal Rangers regularly, worked on projects, and went to events. I kept scrupulous lists of everything that I needed to do to earn advancement patches and medals. A fellow friend and I both received the Silver Medal of Achievement in June 2012 (the former second highest award back then).

Now onto the final mission: the prestigious Gold Medal of Achievement. One of the required merits that I had to earn was First Aid—CPR.

Toward the end of my junior year at Newport Harbor High School, in the spring of 2012, I barely heard "CPR" in the morning announcements. Since nobody else really listens to the morning announcements over the intercom anyway and chatters instead, it was difficult to make out exactly what was being said.

However, I *knew* that I needed to be CPR certified to earn the Gold Medal of Achievement for Royal Rangers. (In the summer of 2011, my mother and I were looking to take a CPR class together but ended up not doing it.) I subsequently deliberated with myself about it. Should I or should I not gather more information? Once class ended that day, I decided to take on the mission to find out about it. I went to the offices and library first and found out that I should go to the career center.

The class, called "Emergency Medical Responder" (EMR), was offered by the Regional Occupational Program (ROP). It was Monday through Thursday, 8:00-12:30 and ran from the end of June 2012 until the middle of July. When the morning finally came, I arrived there early. Inside, I was quite nervous because I was waitlisted. I could not even sit at the table outside. I had to stand up and walk toward the fence, breathing in some fresh air.

Finally, after waiting a few minutes past eight for latecomers, the instructor called out the names from the roster. The instructor went back in, presumably counting. He came back outside and called out people from the waitlist. Each name reverberated in my ears. My name was not called, and he went back inside.

Look, I am probably not going to get in, I tried to console myself before hearing the news all at once.

Then, the instructor came back out again to call out a couple more names, and mine was one of them! Flabbergasted, I took the triumphal journey up the ramp and into the classroom.

The next morning, after being seated, it hit my heart like a hammer. I *almost* did not get in. I got this overwhelming feeling of thankfulness inside. However, I did not yet realize the much bigger meaning of this. This class was more than just an ordinary first aid and CPR course—it was Emergency Medical Responder. We became first responders—the first on the scene to provide immediate medical care to the best of our scope of practice: assessing a scene of emergency, patient assessment, trauma management, triage, airway adjuncts, supplemental oxygen, suctioning, bleeding management, immobilizing/splinting, administering CPR, using an AED, and more.

This class is highly recommended to take right before taking Emergency Medical Technician (EMT), which I am still pondering on pursuing. It is somewhat the preparation for becoming an EMT. Nevertheless, there were larger blessings up ahead, and these are told in other short stories in this anthology.

I successfully passed this course and was certified by the American Heart Association. (I later got re-certified as an EMR two years later at Orange Coast College.) *Phew!*

Previously, at the beginning of junior year, I decided to become an elementary school teacher. The passions were *tenacious*! Less than a year later, I had an equal passion for getting into the medical field because of being an EMR. Furthermore, if my mother and I ended up taking a regular First Aid/CPR class, then I might not have been inspired to get into the medical field. If it were not for Royal Rangers, I probably would not have such an aspiration at all. Since 2012, I have carried a first aid kit in my pocket just in case someone needs help in the community. It used to be cumbersomely bulky, but after a few years, I simply started carrying a homemade, pocket-sized one.

Nonetheless, I *still* have a teaching passion. (You will read in a couple other short stories about what I decided to do and a greater reward of even taking an ROP class, but bear in mind that Royal Rangers made it happen.)

I still had a few more requirements for the GMA while concurrently, I was finishing up my final year of high school. By 2013, I came up with three merits: Juggling, Advanced Juggling, and Human Anatomy and had written out all the requirement in detail. In 2014, I sent my ideas to the national office in Missouri, so one day, there might be merits that I designed being circulated all around the world. You never know. (I designed a coin for economics class in twelfth grade. After a friend of mine mailed my design to the U.S. Mint, I got an official letter from them—watermark and all. The entire story about it almost made *The Beacon*, the school newspaper.)

By May 2013, I was on a direct path toward earning the Gold Medal of Achievement. In the interim, I turned in my final, sentimental work for the last merits that I could ever obtain before formally graduating from Expedition Rangers, which, again, is the concluding division.

Just for being me, I wanted to get at least *one* silver merit. These are for the Expedition Rangers and are more advanced, high school level merits. I browsed through the ones that were offered and chose Economics. I had gotten a B in my economics class earlier that year. I looked at the requirements and referred to the notes that I took, along with additional research. Now, I have a silver merit on my awards vest (the uniform). In total, I have earned 96 merits.

Contrary to popular belief, I did *not* earn every single one that is offered! In fact, Royal Rangers offers over three hundred total merits. Five days before turning eighteen, I turned in my final papers for the Gold Medal. It was categorically official. It was not a dream.

On Sunday, September 8, 2013, my friend and I had a complete, formal Gold Medal of Achievement Court of Honor. It was held inside Needham Chapel at Vanguard University by Newport Mesa Church. Innumerable friends and family came. A couple of my former commanders who used to volunteer at my outpost came in and spoke.

My friend and I both received a myriad of letters from dignitaries at the district and national offices of Royal Rangers, as well as a United States Senator. The day before, I was given a letter from Dr. George O. Wood, the General Superintendent of the Assemblies of God (I got to meet him in person on September 28, 2014).

Needless to say the obvious, I am blessed to be in Royal Rangers. It was God's working that directed my mother to go to that church in Lomita and hear about Royal Rangers. Then, it was her meeting the friend who would eventually find this outpost for me; even that is an incredible story.

Royal Rangers had become my life's passion. I knew that I *always* wanted to be a part of the program for decades after receiving the GMA. I am thankful beyond words put together in a library of novels.

Immediately, I wanted to give back with all my heart.

2

Being a Royal Rangers' Commander

At the after-party of my Gold Medal of Achievement Court of Honor on September 8, 2013, I reminded the senior commander that I wanted to come back to help out. The new academic year started the following Wednesday. He said that he placed me with the Ranger Kids. (Again, that is K-2nd.)

Therefore, on Wednesday, September 11, 2013, I returned to Newport Mesa Church in full uniform and began my first day ever as a lieutenant commander. I was elated and jubilant.

I became overwhelmed with dedication, and joy. I firmly believe that this is where God has placed me at this point in life. Remember my tenacious passion to teach children in the previous short story? Well, this is simply a good, quintessential beginning!

On that night, I was asked to do a devotion spontaneously for the Ranger Kids. At my outpost, I have shared an abundance of devotions. No joke, but I had to deliver several of them with minutes and even seconds to prepare. If the person does not show up, or they need somebody quickly, I am the guy they ask. I have also been the person in charge of teaching the older boys how to give a devotion so that they could deliver one for the younger boys.

By September 2014, I became a full-fledged commander and was completely in charge of the second grade. A little less than a month after I became a commander, one of my favorite, former commanders from Buckaroos passed away, succumbing to cancer. He was not a commander there at the time, but it was hard to get over the emptiness. I always saw him at another church. He kept getting weaker but always had a smile on his face. I attended his funeral service that November.

It is still a little hard getting over the loss, but I remember spending a lot of fun times with him. I remember looking through a telescope that he brought over one night and also recall him showing us a hundred dollar bill that he would give to anyone who could put all the toothpaste that we squeezed out back inside the tube.

A lot of outposts use drill commands and formations. Toward the latter years in Royal Rangers, our outpost did not enforce them. In the spring of 2015, I studied and memorized the drill commands for formation and marching, such as "Fall in," "Dress right, dress," "Parade rest," "Ready, two," and others. I asked the head commander of the Ranger Kids if I could teach the drill commands properly to them. He granted me the leeway and subsequently, all of the Ranger Kids got it down remarkably. Therefore, I had officially started the drill commands for the Ranger Kids, and they had fun doing it. Thus, I strive to have the entire outpost follow them too one day, because if the youngest division could do it, then so can everybody.

Meanwhile, I was put in charge of reviving our Color Guard/Flag Retirement team. We officially initiated the patrol system in the fall of 2016 for the Discovery Rangers, in order to have the boys implement leadership responsibility. This is one of the crucial aspects of the entire program. In the fall of 2017, the

Discovery Rangers got the drill commands down pat. Two down, two to go.

By 2017, I had completed most of the commander's training, hosted by the district, including World Class Outpost (WCO) in 2015, which was a huge, two-day, advanced training course.

Needless to say, I love further maximizing my effectiveness as a commander for these "young men" via continual learning and training. I endeavor to be the best I can be, all the while fulfilling what God calls me to be.

Furthermore, besides helping to teach merits and such, I love to contribute my artistic creativity to the outpost. I designed the "Ranger Bucks" for a few years and incorporated a lot of detail in them. In 2017, I created four big posters to encourage all the four divisions of Royal Rangers into earning merits and advancing on their "trail." They are visualizations of their advancements. When a boy earns the next rank, the commander will move their name tags closer to the medals that they are working on. It is a tool to keep everybody aware of where everybody else is on the advancement trail. This should hopefully impart the same amount of excitement that I had while working on merits during free time.

In total, it must have taken hundreds of hours of designing, going to places, and contacting several people before finding the perfect place to have them printed. Finally, the three foot by four-and-a-half-foot posters arrived via UPS on April 26, 2017. So far, everybody's been loving them, and I had planned to send my idea to the national office in Missouri.

Royal Rangers has been the most incredible experience in my entire life, to say the least. To date, I have had just under two decades of nostalgic memories in the program, and I will continue to always remain in it. I will never forget all my thirteen years in the program before becoming a commander. I will neither forget walking around Vanguard University one night with my fellow Buckaroos or hearing that wild owl one night at Lake Hemet in an April 2013 campout. Neither will I forget throwing tomahawks and knives or the campouts that I have been on. I will never forget all the excellent, amiable commanders. I will always remember the leadership I learned and am learning. I cherish every nanosecond of it!

Currently, as of publishing this anthology, I am in my twentieth year in Royal Rangers and have been a commander since that first day in 2013. Now, I am teaching boys (i.e., future men and future leaders) with the skills that I was taught before they were even born! Plus, I am teaching and facilitating new skills and knowledge.

I have thus far taught the Astronomy merit, Tool Craft, Compass, and Weather, among a few others. I further assisted with Bible merits, leadership merits, Archery, and Lashing, to name a few. In the future, I aspire to teach a myriad more.

In addition to being called to do the devotions (even at the last minute) and being referred to as the "knot expert," I am also known as the "first aid man." I have rendered first aid a lot of times in the past few years of being a commander; consequently, I teach the First Aid Skills merit.

I cannot say it enough, but I do not know where I would be in my life without Royal Rangers. I told one of the pastors at Newport Mesa Church, as well as commanders, that if it were up to me, I would be volunteering at Royal Rangers seven days a week. I told that to the Discovery Rangers, and some of them wished the same thing.

Am I forgetting anything? Oh, yes. I have Asperger's syndrome so I am intrinsically shy, inherently bashful, and innately timid. While these hindrances *do* get in the way, I have overcome most of it, as well as a lot of my other challenging symptoms of Asperger's. (As you read through this anthology, you will know and understand how I cannot help some of these issues that many of us who suffer autism go through. However, you will see how day-by-day and year-by-year, I have gotten over many of them.)

After all the implementations and experiences with leadership and being a commander over diligent young boys, things have been getting easier and easier for me. Moreover, my awards vest has been allowing me to introduce Royal Rangers to hundreds of people. Several passersby always come over and ask me about my vest, and I get the pleasure of telling them about the third biggest blessing in my life. I have invited several parents and children to come check us out and will continue to do so.

Whenever I am wearing my awards vest outside of Royal Rangers, I receive endless compliments. They remind me of how much dedication that I must have had in order to be wearing it. Without that vest, truthfully, I do not think that I would have the same confidence that I get while wearing it. It helps me break out of my cockamamie nervousness and hold conversations with new people. I get to share Royal Rangers and importantly share about God and what He has done for me in my life (and what He is *continually* doing).

Every person with autism needs such confidence. I found it *partly* through the vest that God has blessed me with; other people find it elsewhere. (Just to be clear, I do not always wear it everywhere I go.)

Regardless, I am thankful for what is *represented* by the vest—the things that people remind me of: dedication, passion, hard work, perseverance, endurance, and loyalty. *That* is what I want everyone to see, and *not* something that would make them jealous or give up. That is never my intention. Rather, I want it to be something to *inspire* and *encourage.*

Through the vest, I have already become an inspiration and encouragement to hundreds if not thousands of people, even outside the United States. (I have found that out over time.) My thrill is to motivate children into realizing what *they* can accomplish.

Essentially, if I could be an Eagle Scout equivalent—while having Asperger's syndrome—then undoubtedly, millions of other people could do it too.

Furthermore, I want everybody in the community to recognize that I am willing to help people, especially children, in both learning and skills, such as science and mathematics, or tying knots and using a compass.

I am *always* thankful for Royal Rangers and what it has taught me.

I am *always* thankful for my commanders who helped me and never gave up on me, even though I am a person who naturally juggled tough issues.

I will *always* support Royal Rangers.

I will *always* promote it and recommend it to everyone who asks.

I will *always* be a commander.

I want *every* child worldwide to benefit from the program that I most benefitted from!

Importantly, I give *all* credit, praise, and glory to God. Without Him, none of this could have been possible.

3

SPEECH DELAY AND IMPEDIMENT

My mother used to be only one of a couple of people who could understand me when I spoke. One day, a friend of the family recommended that I get evaluated for it. I was subsequently diagnosed with a speech delay problem when I was about three.

Consequently, I was enrolled in the Preschool Intervention Program. I began preschool in September 1999 at College Park Elementary School. The school bus picked me up in front of the house; I still remember the names of a couple of my bus drivers from that year.

As soon as class began, the first part of our day was playing in a designated area of the classroom. On certain days, during our playtime, one to two ladies would walk in with big smiles. They came to take me and a couple others to speech class. Hard to believe, I loathed having to go to speech class because I had to put down what I was playing with and go to a small room elsewhere. Nonetheless, I loved it in the years after that. The fun games that we would play had us engage in conversations and asking questions. This aided in improving all of our speech. One of my favorite games was Mystery Garden.

In Kindergarten and first grade, I really had to work on my G's, S's, and Th's. "Go" would sound like "Doe" and "Great" as "Drate." I would also mix up the S sounds with the Th sounds, pronouncing "Sound" as "Thound," "Swing" as "Thwing," "Three" as "Free," and "This" as "Fis."

After perseverance and pronunciation drills, I got the hang of my G's after Kindergarten. During first grade, my former kindergarten teacher would come by and take me to her classroom after lunch on certain days. There would be a booklet where each page had four simple illustrations of arbitrary objects. Each page was divided into four quadrants (one object per quadrant).

One day, I surprised her by correctly pronouncing my G's all of a sudden. Within a moment or two, she turned the page, and one of the illustrations was a gift-wrapped box with a bow on top. I got jubilant.

"Present," she pointed when we came to it.

"Present," I repeated. "Or, *gift*."

How I remember it, she gasped in astonishment, leaned back a little, widened her eyes, and smiled. Mission accomplished. Now, it was onto my S's and Th's. I did not quite achieve the correct pronunciation of those until fifth or sixth grade. After that, nevertheless, I occasionally mispronounced words. I just further practiced articulating more clearly.

I have not always liked my voice and how I sounded; it was one overwhelming thing that seemed to have *always* been in the back of my mind. Some people seemed annoyed with it, and that was personally exasperating to me. My grandfather and mother regularly took thousands of pictures and hundreds of hours of home videos. As I re-watch these videos, *I* find it hard to understand myself here and there. I end up having to decipher what I was saying.

My voice sounded as if I were shivering in freezing temperatures; some of my words were elongated. I felt that once a person heard my voice for the first time, they would assume that there was something abnormal. I dreaded that I might not ever talk or sound like everybody else. It also became awkward when I suddenly became the loudest person in the crowd. People then turned to stare at me, but I cannot be certain of the reason. Is it because of my impediment, or am I saying something interesting?

Contrariwise, I will never forget a couple of times when people asked me, "Where are you from?" They thought that my impediment was an accent. I took those as compliments.

The older I grew and simply practiced talking, the more times my friends did not have to ask me to repeat what I said. That had gotten frustrating now and again. Additionally, the words "uh" and "um" have been infiltrating into my sentences for several years, but I have practiced enough to limit those interruptions as well.

While teaching or giving an answer, my goal is to speak confidently and without stuttering. I *prepare* for questions. I may know the answer, but I might need a few seconds processing the question and recalling how to answer it in the most concise way. I suppose that I endeavor to be like doctors, firefighters, or somebody else in a career that requires running on adrenaline. If an emergency happens, they know what to do in a heartbeat. When teachers are asked questions, they usually answer in a snap of the fingers. I aspire and practice to be like that one day.

By high school and college, many people told me that they could not tell that I have an impediment. Plus, people said that they could see me neither being an R.S.P. (Resource Specialist Program) student nor requiring special accommodations. Nevertheless, I cannot hide this frustrating problem, but I got better via perseverance. If I did not have early intervention such as preschool and speech therapy, then this would be a different story. It is immensely critical for these to be applied as early as possible.

Since I have personally never given up, I can enunciate not impeccably, but at least more clearly.

4

Novel-Long Conversations

I am intrinsically quite talkative. I can go on and on for hours if I get too carried away.

Having Asperger's syndrome, it is quite common for me not to maintain eye contact. Some of us force it, which may inadvertently make whomever we are talking to uncomfortable. I have taken notice of this and accordingly endeavored to implement proper eye contact.

I merely do not know whether the person with whom I am talking is trying to decipher what I am saying or if that is just how he or she listens. Some people make different facial expressions in order to understand me more clearly despite my impediment. I have since learned how to tell if they are.

On the other hand, when the person with whom I am talking does not have eye contact with me, I sometimes wonder whether or not he or she is distracted.

"Are they engaged?" I ask myself. "Or are they bored? Am I just babbling their ear off?"

I find that when the person looks away from me ever so slightly, I do feel a smidgen more comfortable. When they are not staring at me the whole entire time, it is a few moments of regrouping. The conversation feels more casual (even though most of the time, it already is). However, I may cease eye contact myself until I see in my peripheral vision that he or she is looking back up to me; a split second later, I will look back at them.

I suppose I try to balance it. As I explain things, I use my hands and arms a lot to supplement my words. When I speak, I notice that I start to nonchalantly look away, even though I know the proper etiquette of eye contact. In the middle of a sentence or paragraph, I might look at a distant object or the sky for concentration. Characteristically, I find myself looking back and forth between a person and the intricate details of something, such as objects or the patterns of carpeting or upholstery. Whether I am holding a conversation with somebody (in person or on the phone) or rehearsing alone, I can frequently recall what was previously talked about whenever I refocus on an object or pattern. For instance, if I see a picture on a wall at one point while talking to somebody and look back at it later on, I can remember what I was talking about when I first saw it. Quite often, it gives me déjà vu. While it evokes what was being said at the time, I still have my attention on what is being said at the present. In essence, I do not lose too much focus.

To reiterate, I have always been very loquacious. If I do not catch it immediately, I can literally talk for a *long* time. I love talking, but conversations need to be more dialogue than monologue. I have further practiced the vital conversational skill of giving others time to speak by limiting details. I ask questions to prevent my dominating the conversation.

I am the sole conductor of several trains of thoughts. I get nervous when I suddenly lose one of them from out of nowhere, or if a name or date escapes my mind for a few moments. Now and again, I do not remember until right after leaving. At any nanosecond, the person with whom I am talking can either give his or her response before I am finished or end the dialogue. The longer another person speaks once he or she started, the more I formulate answers in response. Sometimes, I may have to retain ten or twenty things in my mind simultaneously before the next time I get the chance to speak. I accordingly have become more conscious of when I tend to dominate conversations, for that is probably how it felt for others.

During twelfth grade, a member of the staff of Newport Harbor High School took notice of my long-winded explanations over simple things. He pointed it out to me and suggested that I keep it short and simple. *Short* and *simple*!

I basically do not need to recite a book. He said that if people want more details, then they would ask for them. We practiced together. I may not remember word-for-word, but I started talking about the fire alarm.

"The fire alarm is super, super loud. It comes out of nowhere and is quite startling. It *really* needs to be turned down like at my other school…" (This is the essence of what I was saying).

He cut me off sometime around there. He pointed out that I was about to go on and on again. He suggested that I simply say, "The first alarm is very loud." That is all. If an explanation is needed, then people will ask for it. Just stick to the heart of the story.

As I left that day, I considered what I was just taught. It was during third period, and long story short, I did not have a third period class most of my senior year. Therefore, I went to the school's library and sat down at one of the tables. Two friends of mine came up to me and asked how my weekend was.

I said something like, "It was very special," bearing in mind what had just been recommended to me to do (even though it was hard). I may or may not have added a small detail or two, but not much if I did.

My friend asked me how it was special. That moment stuck out to me. Success! It worked.

Instead of thoroughly giving every last detail at the start, I broke it up. I realized how much more decorous it is to shorten what I say. Again, it is hard for me. If memory serves me correctly, I gave a short reply, and my friend asked another question for additional details.

The people with whom I am talking may only have a few minutes. Anything over that, and they may just be tolerating the time I spend going on and on. They might then take a mental note for the next time they approach me, considering whether or not to have a conversation.

Nowadays, when I run into people, I sometimes discern when they are busy. This leads to an important note that I did not yet say. Sociably, due to Asperger's, I am nervous about going up to people to begin with. I have often waited for people to come up to me and start the conversation. High school was when my advocacy exponentially skyrocketed. For four years, my RSP teacher taught us to be self-advocates with the ability to speak for ourselves instead of relying on others to speak for us. Though I'm still nervous now, it was not as before, albeit, it still persists to some degree.

If I can tell when another person is not busy, I can easily initiate the conversation myself. The continual implementation of advocacy has extremely helped me with this. I now feel more comfortable to go up to people, which is really helping me out in college. Otherwise, I just wait...and wait...and wait. I loathe interrupting people when they are either busy or talking to someone. Even best friends. Once I am officially in a conversation, my main stresses (other than utilizing the correct amount of eye contact and inflection) are to both prove that I am listening, as well as to match my facial expression according to what is expected. This is as difficult as trying to talk in the dialogue in the first place.

"How am I supposed to look and act?" I apprehensively ask myself as I attempt to pick up on cues. I try my absolute best to match my countenance with how I feel. I do not want my facial expressions to make people assume that I am uninterested or bored with the conversation. As certain people talk to me, I start wondering if they are thinking, "Are you even listening to me, Matthew? Do you understand what I'm saying?"

I do! (That is, if my mind is not distracting me by talking louder than the person. Other than that, I am still listening attentively.) I am most likely using trial and error to find the conforming look. If I start to smile in any way, I could inadvertently make the person feel rushed.

"Do I look puzzled when I'm trying to look sympathetic?" I ask myself, among other emotions.

There are times when I think that something is interesting or that a joke is funny, yet people are like, "He doesn't get it." Sometimes, they say that verbally; and consequently, I spend about a minute attempting to prove that I sincerely understand it and am paying attention.

Additionally, when others somehow think that I am exhausted—but am nonetheless following along—I might be asked, "Are you okay?" or "Falling asleep there, buddy?"

So what about other kinds of conversations—those that I *find* myself in?

Some friends of mine talk about things that I absolutely cannot relate to or joke about things that I do not find humorous. When people do that, employ slang I don't understand, or give me a hard time, I completely do not know how to respond. It is as if my brain is a malfunctioning machine that vibrates with smoke coming out. Some of them laugh out loud as a result of my sudden timidity.

Every time after talking with somebody, my mind reverberates the parts that stuck out to me. I subsequently wonder when the next opportunity to chat with someone—anyone—would be.

Considering all the procedures of proficiently holding a conversation, it can be quite enervating. I plan to continue getting even better while conversing with others and minimize stuttering. And I intend to have fun doing so. For a person with Asperger's syndrome, I am already quite blessed to be able to implement advocacy as much as I can. For many years now, I have utilized responsibility. I started conversations on my own with friends, went up to my teachers and professors, did my banking, shopping, and more.

It is a great feeling to be taken into someone's confidence. At the same time, it is numbing. I am on my own. It is as if I am trying to balance one foot on the spire of a skyscraper. I do not have a person over my shoulder to confirm what I am saying is suitable for that specific time. That is what practice and apprenticeship are for. I shadowed not only my family, teachers, and friends, but also certain moral characters on television and in the movies (whether real or fiction).

> *Let your speech be always with grace, seasoned with salt, that ye may know how ye ought to answer every man* (Colossians 4:6).

Just as juggling gets easier with practice, so shall holding conversations and advocacy be for everybody.

5

The Melodious Tranquility of Music

The door opened, and I rushed inside the condominium where the welcoming fragrance of the eucalyptus wreath greeted me. I sat down at the piano bench and started tickling the ivories.

I was in Fullerton, California, visiting friends when I was probably around seven or eight years old. My mother had been taking me over there since I was born. The couple, Tom and Ginny Carr, were co-authors of a book, and Ginny was a musician.

Almost every time when I visited, I would play their piano, even though I had no clue what I was doing. I was simply getting familiar with the pitches of its eighty-eight keys. This greatly inspired me. At a young age, I wanted to learn how to play.

Thus, Tom and Ginny paid for a keyboard after school program for me. In third grade, at Newport Heights Elementary School, I learned the basics of the keyboard. At the graduation party on April 30, 2004, all the students who took the program got to choose a song or two and perform it. I would say that was my first actual keyboard/piano performance. I took keyboard classes a few times at Newport Heights Elementary too. After I learned the basics, everything else was predominantly self-taught.

I continued to practice and practice and practice. I tried to compose my own songs and melodies, in addition to playing songs by ear. I utilized perseverance and never gave up.

In fourth grade, I performed in my first school talent show. It was jubilating. I was excited for weeks. When the curtains opened, I heard roars of applause. After persistently practicing beforehand, I played "God Bless America." In fact, I was in more than one show. There were one or two shows in the day, followed by one at night. In each of the shows that I played in, I smiled at the audience, then turned toward the keyboard. Closing my eyes, I played the first notes. Then I opened my eyes, and it was as if I were alone rehearsing. That helped me overcome any potential nervousness. Notwithstanding, it was fun! In the following year, I entered the talent show again and played "Ode to Joy."

In seventh grade, a friend from California Victory Church (it has since been renamed Victory Church OC) gave me a harmonica. It was not my first one, but it came with the song, "When the Saints Go Marching In." Accordingly, I began playing the harmonica for real.

In eighth grade U.S. History and Geography class, on December 12, 2008, my teacher allowed me to play "Old Folks at Home" by Stephen Foster on my harmonica. We were just learning about "the father of American music" in our studies.

When I came home from school one day, probably back in seventh grade, my grandfather came out and made sure that I had my eyes closed. He guided me through the door and pointed me in the direction toward the couch. When I opened my eyes, my cousin was there smiling and holding up an electric guitar. I became flabbergasted.

The same friend who gave me the harmonica at church started giving me guitar lessons, which lasted all throughout eighth grade. She and I would work with the children's church and performed in front of the congregation a couple of times. Soon, another student joined us in guitar lessons, and she was a beautiful singer. In 2009, the three of us prepared for a Valentine's Day concert at Flagship Health Care Center in Newport Beach.

Despite learning how to play all these instruments, there was one thing that I just could not do. Singing has always been my major dilemma. Because of my impediment, I cannot carry a tune. I have *always* had a zeal to sing, but I mostly sang to myself. Nevertheless, I know lots of songs and have memorized the verses of a couple, including "Come Thou Fount of Every Blessing" and "How Deep the Father's Love for Us." In sixth grade, I knew the three verses of "This Land Is Your Land," and I would sing it to myself all the time.

I always pondered about winning *American Idol*, hoping that my voice would finally get to normal by the time I became an adult. However, I may be better off competing in *Dancing with the Stars*. I still cannot carry a tune. Therefore, I would not want to go on the show and bear the responsibility of shattering everybody's television screens via my cacophonous singing voice.

To this day, however, I still really wish to sing. A worship leader at St. Andrew's Presbyterian Church insists, "Sure you can!" Well, I know I *can* sing…just not harmoniously. I had to sing during guitar lessons twice, but when the third opportunity came, I refused. I was too nervous. I knew I could not do it. This is not a case of giving up on something. Unless God will supernaturally give me a singing voice one morning, I *cannot* sing *well*. He simply had called me into other areas of worship, like instruments. For that, I am grateful.

During rehearsals for a play I was in, back in 2006, I was practicing with some of the other cast members on one of the songs. Number one, I was standing toward the bass end of the piano and was shadowing the pianist's skill of playing. Anyway, the pianist kept on stopping because she was detecting something that was off key. It was my voice. I was simply throwing everybody off, especially her. After a few times of inadvertent interruptions, I was officially kicked out of the choir and stuck with acting. (The play was *Cinderella,* and I played Prince Charming. At least I learned how to dance the waltz.)

I did, in fact, sing in a small choir once. After a few months of rehearsing, I sang in a Christmas program for the Trinity Broadcasting Network (TBN) on Sunday, December 14, 2008. Alas, something happened, and it never aired on television.

I have been surrounded by music all of my life. There is simply something unexplainable about music that tenaciously grasps me. I like several songs and soundtracks. Some of my favorites came from music class at school, some from the theme songs of television shows, some came from cassette tapes, and some came from movies. Nonetheless, I cannot sing like most other people. A big reason why there are several songs that I can only hear at certain times is that I feel left out and excluded.

Upon listening to certain songs, I panic. I feel as if I am breathing through a straw, for my breathing becomes labored. Sometimes, I have to resort to a near-tripod position. The other big reason is nostalgia and bashfulness, but that is a long story. Simply, music could quickly bring me back to my childhood, even though some songs were written in recent years, while others were written decades before I was born.

Since I probably will not be capable of singing melodiously, I converted all of my strong singing passions to piano playing, which is why piano playing is extremely important in my life. I play piano in lieu of singing. It is my way of cathartically releasing my desire to perform music for others. It is like choosing the best alternative. Even practicing by myself is a release of tension and emotion, but playing it in front of several people is the culmination.

In the long run, I dedicated more time and practice to the piano. If I cannot sing, I will pursue piano. I adamantly believe that God has been blessing me through this talent.

In fact, before I was born, my mother called in on a radio station. If she had never done that, this short story may never have been written. My mother got to talk to Joni Eareckson Tada. She was a special guest just for that night. Afterward, Joni had her assistant call Tom and Ginny Carr in Fullerton to ask them to contact my mother. The three of them met, which is how they became friends.

Shortly after, Ginny called my mother and offered her a housekeeping job because their former housekeeper had quit. My mother, a nonmedical healthcare provider and housekeeper, started working for them regularly at their condominium, and she still works for Ginny to this day. (Tom passed away in 2007.) As time went on, my mother got to meet Joni in person. I was later born in 1995, and the rest is history.

Additionally, the story of how Tom and Ginny got married almost never happened. Their incredible, suspenseful story is all told in their book that they published in 1989: *Waiting Hearts: A Story of Extraordinary Love.* I read it in 2012. I loved it so much that I reread it the next year. I knew them, of course, so there was a deeper significance to the story. We firmly believe that God has designed it to be this way; He had everything happen the way it did.

I am ready! That is who I am as a Royal Ranger. Always ready. Nearly every time when I walk by a piano, I am very tempted to play it. In all the churches where I have been attending since 2010, I have always anticipated the worship leader coming over to me and requesting that I play something at the last minute. I almost *always* carry sheet music on me, even when we go to the grocery store or other errands. I never know where a piano could possibly be hiding, even in transit to and from errands.

It became frustrating when I finally had the opportunity to play, but I did not bring any music with me. Thus, I nearly always carry sheet music now.

In the interim, I met one of the pianists of St. Andrew's Presbyterian after church one Sunday. Throughout the rest of high school, she and the worship leader of the church gave me tips sporadically. This helped me improve significantly.

In November 2012, after the high school youth group adjourned, that same worship leader called my name. For some reason, I figured that he was finally going to ask me to play the piano. I just discerned that in my heart. No joke, I was right, for I had it confirmed a few seconds later.

"I was wondering if you want to play three stanzas of 'How Deep The Father's Love For Us' this Sunday," he asked.

I became ecstatic. I, of course, said, "Sure! I'd be honored to."

The next Sunday, I played this favorite song of mine in a prelude solo right before church started. Only a percentage of the congregation was there, but it was fun nonetheless.

A year or two earlier, I had told another worship leader from the youth group that I was interested in joining the band. He wrote down my name and that I would be willing to play either harmonica or keyboard. My passion is to play *with* people. My ultimate goal was to play with the band in both the youth group and the main services. I was told that I could, eventually.

Unfortunately, it never happened exactly that way. In the youth group, I only got to play a couple of preludes while everybody else was walking in and chattering loudly.

Finally, I had to be more assertive. I have Asperger's syndrome. It is difficult for autistic people like myself to do so. Putting my foot in the door makes me feel weird inside. I feel like a five-year-old bossing around an experienced, fifty-year-old professional. I feel like a new film director directing movie veterans. Notwithstanding, I am a person who endeavors to *overcome* the issues of Asperger's. High school was the time in my life where I implemented advocacy.

On April 10, 2012, I was filmed by one of the youth leaders explaining a picture that I painted about Jesus; it was to be shown on the sixteenth. That same morning, I messaged one of the worship leaders requesting "In Christ Alone" to be played on the sixteenth, as well as if it is possible for me to play "How Deep The Father's Love For Us" on the keyboard. *Enter*, I pressed on the computer's keyboard. It was simply no longer a time for me to be reticent.

On the evening of Monday, April 16, 2012, I got to play that song on the keyboard after the video. The worship leader led the vocals and played his guitar. Finally, I got to play with someone in front of my peers. I would have sung to, but I did not want to bust the speakers with my discordant cacophony of singing.

I scrupulously started to get the major and minor chords mastered by 2012. I was getting closer in realizing how piano music is actually played. In retrospect, I began considering that it was probably a good thing that I did not start playing in the youth group's band right away. I spent December 2012 and early 2013 self-teaching myself and practicing the major and minor chords. Soon, I nearly became a pro at it. Then one day, I started breaking up basic chords by serendipity. I played it for the pianist of St. Andrew's Presbyterian. She asked me if I knew what that was called.

"No," I replied.

"Arpeggio."

Since then, I have practiced a few different techniques of arpeggio, as I continued to implement reading sheet music.

Truthfully, I am not Beethoven, Chopin, Bach, or Mozart. I cannot read those types of sheet music. To this day, as long as I have a treble clef and the chords written above it, I can probably play it after practicing (provided that it is in a relatively easy key, such as C, D, Eb, F, and G major, as well as E minor). Sometimes, it just takes practicing the song once or twice straight through, and then I master it.

Certain pieces of music, however, get stuck in my head. Moreover, I can instantly recall other songs if I read or hear a couple of arbitrary words that happen to be found in its lyrics. Songs characteristically evoke various epochs. I can instantly receive the warm feelings of the forties and fifties while listening to certain sentimental music. Others, it is the sixties, seventies, eighties, or nineties. There are melodies from the 1700s and 1800s that I adore as well. Then there are nostalgic songs that literally grab onto me and transport me back to my days as a kindergartener, first and second grader, fourth grader, middle schooler, and so on. It is analogous to how certain aromas can take a person back several years.

Since I started getting better at piano playing, I reopened my request to play at both the youth group and the main service. I was not talking about playing preludes, rather to play with the band, plus offertory solos. Perhaps one year, I would be equipped to play during St. Andrew's Presbyterian's big, annual Christmas concerts too.

Months after I graduated high school, I still had not been able to play music with others. After asking, the high school director messaged me back and said that he prefers to have the high schoolers be involved in the entire worship team, and through this, it should encourage a better, more significant youth group. Hoping that everything will be led by the high schoolers, he appended that if the keys are unavailable for one night, then it will be offered to another high schooler. If there is not a high schooler available, then one of the small group leaders will be asked. *And*, if by *some* happenstance, that *nobody* could play keys, *then*, they would surely let me know! Fantastic! Now I just have to wait some more for that improbability to occur. I had only been waiting for a few years at that point. Oh, swell.

I nearly had a heart attack upon reading that reply. I was like a doctor who spent years in medical school and kept getting rejected by every hospital that he applied to. I strictly kept requesting to be a "*volunteer.*" I believe that I emphasized that word in my question. I do not need to be paid to play piano for a church. Truthfully, I am not sure if that was what it was or not.

Not letting this stop me, I started playing for Victory Fellowship OC here and there but mostly solos. There was a couple of times when I got to play with a small band. Additionally, I got to play in the entire band one Sunday morning at California Victory Church in 2014. It was a further experience of playing *with* others—praising and worshiping *together*. Then, I was going to do it again later, but right when church started, some of the power went out. The keyboard happened to be one of them, if not the only one. I literally could not play. It was very disconcerting.

I still firmly believe that God has been calling me into

music—specifically piano/keyboard—among a few other gifts. Throughout 2014, I played a medley for the WMA (Worship Musicians Association) three times at California Victory Church. In each of those times, I was also volunteering in the sound booth and putting up the lyrics for everybody.

Now, this is imperative to take note of: on May 30, 2014, my first time ever performing for the WMA, I received a word from God. After I played the keyboard, I went back up to the sound booth. Roughly three-quarters of an hour later, a couple of people went on stage. While the instruments were being set up, one of them was talking when she suddenly said, "I believe your name's Matthew? Is that correct?" This is the actual transcript of what followed:

> "As you were on the keys over here, you know, I just saw God the Father just sitting in this big couch. And just in such delight and breathing in the aroma of your worship. It was absolutely beautiful. Keep going. Keep moving forward because you're anointed, and God wants to use you."

Everybody started clapping and praising God right at that point. After the WMA, I got to meet her. She said that she saw it as "clear as day." That night was further confirmation to me that I am called to play piano and that I will be playing in front of many people one day. The entire church was packed on this night. There were at least between one and two hundred people.

Music is cathartic for me and helps me focus. If I just need a break from the current stresses that I face, I sometimes begin playing my keyboard or a piano app on my touchscreen laptop. Occasionally, I happen to be near an actual piano.

Since I am now a member of Newport Mesa Church, I will hopefully start to play there on Sunday mornings; even once a month would suffice. Meanwhile, I simply prayed to get such an opportunity to play for a church. And then it happened! In August 2017, the senior pastor of Newport Mesa Church introduced me via Facebook to another local pastor who was in desperate need for a person who could play hymns on the piano. I gave this local pastor a list of over thirty hymns that I could play. On August 20, 2017, I started volunteering weekly at a small church service for the senior citizens of the community instead of Newport Mesa Church. It has just been very peaceful to revive these cherished songs and to have the congregation sing along. Additionally, through this opportunity, I have improved as a piano player, especially in technique and timing.

This has been an answer to prayer, and I am thankful that the senior pastor at Newport Mesa recommended me. I have been waiting since about 2010 to play in front of a church on a regular basis.

On my own YouTube channel, I have scores of piano music that I recorded over the years. I publish them to bless people who want to listen. Also on YouTube, I published videos regarding my personal, firsthand experience of autism to encourage families and individuals. Because of those Autism Awareness Month videos that I shared in April 2018, I was invited to speak on my experiences at a church in Placentia, California, that April.

I am definitely not impeccable at piano playing. I try my best, and that is all that I can do. I pray and ask God to guide my hands as I perform for the enjoyment of others. It is a blessing to be a blessing.

6

JUGGLING AND THE U.S. PRESIDENTS

"Wow, look at that plane!" my aunt pointed at a high-altitude jet on a clear, blue sky day. It was probably one that just departed from LAX. She was watching me while my mother was at work. We were playing catch out in the front yard one day, most likely in early 2006.

My aunt loves airplanes as much as I go crazy over blimps. To no surprise, she went to an airshow one day and brought back souvenirs. One of the items that she got me was what looked like a squeezable baseball with their logo on it.

That is what started me on juggling in the fifth grade. I started tossing it up and down and under my arms and legs. I came up with a routine and incessantly kept practicing it. My friends at Newport Heights Elementary complimented me and added, "You have *fast* reflexes!" for I started moving my arms at high speed.

At Royal Rangers one night during recreation, one of my friends was juggling two balls. One day while I was practicing outside my house, my mind replayed that moment. I emulated how my friend had done it. Soon, I was able to juggle two and came up with a juggling routine. I felt very accomplished. I can now do something else besides keyboard/piano.

Soon it was onto three. I started practicing with three, but I was technically doing two. Then one day, my grandfather essentially told me to get them all in the air. That encouragement got me to try it, and soon I was able to juggle three in a circular motion.

While I practiced juggling outside, I kept receiving a myriad of horn honks and compliments from passersby. One afternoon, when I saw a person riding his bike across the street, I began juggling three. After I dropped one, I looked up, and the bicyclist was in the driveway.

By my good fortune, he happened to be a skilled juggler and gave me tips and showed me some tricks, such as Columns, the Cascade, and the Machine. Via practice and plenty of patience, I soon mastered the first two mentioned; I got the hang of the Machine when I was a bit older.

The next day, the man dropped off a package with three "jugglebugs" in them—one blue, one pink, and one yellow. Jugglebugs are cubed beanbags. That way, they will not bounce off each other when they hit.

By sixth grade, I had dedicated hundreds—if not thousands—of hours to juggling. My friends at school and elsewhere kept encouraging me. By now, I could juggle two in my right hand, then switch, and juggle two in my left.

I soon came up with a giant routine, which smoothly combined a few tricks together like a piano medley. Since my jugglebugs came in three different colors, I color-coded it. Like my smaller routines, each trick had a certain number of catches before I transitioned to the next one.

By 2007, I was persevering to juggle four, as well as three in one hand. Moreover, I was considering juggling for my school's annual talent show but was not confident on juggling four just yet. One day, I was talking to the principal out at the lunch tables about it. He told me, "You should juggle four." Right then and there, I was determined to master four for the talent show. I practiced, never gave up, and got better. (*Anybody* could do that if it is their passion.)

Finally, in February 2007, I juggled in front of my fellow schoolmates in the talent show. It was my first-ever, huge juggling performance. Furthermore, I juggled up to *four*. It was quite momentous, and I received a plethora of compliments. I remember juggling in two shows—one during the day and the other at night. The music that I juggled to was Bruce Springsteen's "Land of Hope and Dreams." (Just the beginning music and opening lyrics).

Not ending my juggling career there, I improved and kept praying for God to continue to help me. I juggled all over, and I mean *all* over. Church, Royal Rangers, parks, and with family, friends, neighbors, and more. I would practice incessantly. If I did not bring stuff to juggle, I would find things to juggle. By eighth grade, I could juggle three basketballs after the mile run in physical education.

While in eighth grade, I was practicing at Pinkley Park. Off in the distance, a man was out with his dog. He saw me juggling and was instantaneously in awe. He slowly walked over with a wonderstruck countenance. It was the same man from a few years prior who had given me the tips and the jugglebugs. I did not recognize him right away, but then I remembered. He was impressed that I was still juggling.

The next day, he dropped off another package containing five new jugglebugs, and shortly afterward, he came by and gave me three clubs. By coincidence, I just happened to be outside my house juggling at the time. I started the clubs by first getting used to the motion of one of them. Next, I would practice alternating hands back and forth. Then, I juggled one club and two jugglebugs in the Cascade motion. After that, I juggled two clubs and one jugglebug. Ultimately, I went to three. It took me only two days from when I started with one to juggle three clubs.

My next talent show came later that academic year. In May 2009, at Ensign Intermediate School, I performed in both shows during third period. When students started pouring inside the gymnasium, class by class, the excitement and nervousness kicked in. By the time I was juggling to the same above mentioned Bruce Springsteen song, I used these nerves to give me a boost.

Back in early elementary school, around first or second grade, I became enthralled with the presidents of the United States and American history. I would watch children's shows based on American history, such as Liberty Kids. My admiration of the presidents mainly started with my big, children's dictionary. In this edition, it only went from George Washington to Bill Clinton. I would look at their pictures over and over again in the designated section toward the back of this dictionary. I also had a book about the presidents too that I would constantly flip through.

I was probably in third or fourth grade when I started drawing all of them based on the portraits in the back of this dictionary. I love drawing, so this was a fun personal project. It was my first series of the U.S. presidents, yet it was certainly *not* my last. Around the same time, I would persistently play on my LeapFrog Quantum Pad. One of the pages had all the presidents on it and came with actual recordings of quotes, trivia, and quizzes. I would test myself repetitively.

On September 4, 2007, my first day of seventh grade—not to mention the first day in a huge middle school with multiple classes—I was introducing myself to everybody in my physical education class. It was my last class of the day. Most (if not all) of them were new people that I had not met before. That felt intimidating for a person like me with Asperger's. Plus, I had previously gotten a wrong, formidable impression about high school back around third grade that frightened me. In early 2004, I would say, I confirmed my preconceived notion while driving by a high school. I saw there were actual bars around the windows. I knew it was a matter of time before I was on the other side, and by seventh grade, I was closer to it.

I know I mentioned something about the presidents to my physical education classmates. At this point, I had seen the presidential portraits so many times forwards and backwards. Suddenly, about everybody seemed to have gotten impressed. Toward the end of class, many fellow students surrounded me and asked a bunch of questions about the presidents. They probably also questioned me about how I knew all of this. The truth is that I started remembering the presidents in order, so I just kept at it.

By the end of seventh grade, I had all their term dates memorized—not just the years—and later, their political parties. Hundreds of times at Ensign Intermediate, several students and staff would tell me a number between one and forty-three (on January 20, 2009, it was officially between one and forty-four). If I were arbitrarily given the number twenty-three, for instance, I would reply, "Benjamin Harrison. March 4, 1889 to March 4, 1893. Republican."

My knowledge of the presidents is actually a significant factor in how I got popular in that school and partly how I made friends. People were introduced to me through my knowledge of the presidents, and that is how conversations started. I did not do it to make friends, but it somewhat became an obsession. I could not stop memorizing. Thanks to the State Quarters Program (1999-2008), I had memorized all the states from Delaware to Hawaii in chronological order.

Years later, probably in 2012, in youth group at St. Andrew's Presbyterian, there was a general Bible quiz night. We were all in groups. Right before they started, one of the leaders interjected at the last second what is spontaneously called the "Matthew Kenslow Rule." This means that each person in a group can answer only once (presumably to keep me from answering all the questions). All my teammates groaned.

On August 29, 2009, right before the advent of my freshman year at Newport Harbor High, I was on the game show *Virtual Memory*, which aired on JCTV and TBN. I went on with two other people from California Victory Church (since renamed Victory Church OC). Before my team was introduced to the audience, the host talked to each one of us beforehand to have us prepared. To this day, I lament that I never mentioned anything about juggling, but I *did* mention about the presidents. By this time, I practically memorized all the states that each president was born in.

The host gave me the name of a president. He was so impressed with my skill that he almost did cartwheels and backflips; I saw him go over and prepare the audience about me. When it was time, I uh...got tongue-tied. A member of the audience called out, "James K. Polk." I knew it but had to think about it for a couple of seconds. Overall, I was a century off. I said 1945 and 1949 instead of *18*45 and *18*49. When we played the DVD for our neighbor, he reassured me, "Everybody knew what you meant."

My team ended up coming in second place...out of two teams! (Figure that one out.)

Once I got to Newport Harbor High School, *everything* proliferated. First off, I performed in every annual talent show in my four years there and always came in the top three.

During freshman year, using diligent perseverance, I started getting five down in a circle. I decided to juggle at California Victory Church's annual International Banquet in December 2010, in lieu of playing the keyboard. Since I had a harmonica holder, I got a wild idea earlier that year. I played the harmonica and juggled simultaneously. When I juggled the clubs, I recited Psalm 91. That night, I received a standing ovation.

Over the years, several people have asked me if I had my jugglebugs with me to give them a miniature performance. Sometimes, I did. They were usually my peers, but sometimes, they were teachers and even substitute teachers. My tenth grade Honors Biology teacher (who later became my twelfth grade health teacher) became quite intrigued and had me juggle for everybody in his class a couple of times.

When I started juggling the trick called the Machine, I told everybody what it was called, and one of the students jokingly replied, "You *are* a machine."

In health class, the teacher said after I performed on the first day, "Now if ever it gets boring in here, or if you're tired, just let me know, and Matthew can come up and juggle for you guys."

Later on that year, when I had a free third period, I went to the school library where one of the history teachers introduced me to one of the English teachers. He was in charge of the school yearbook. The history teacher wanted me to show him what I knew about the presidents. By this time, I had all the president's birthdays and death dates memorized.

The English teacher became awestruck and asked if I would be willing to be in a story for the yearbook, in addition to a video. I became flabbergasted and accepted the offer.

Ever since high school, I primarily used juggling to communicate with others about this vital lesson: You see me up here, now you can do the same. Persevere and never give up. Whatever passion(s) that you are juggling in life, whatever they may be, just keep going for it. And soon, you will be in front of others like me. If you have a disability like me, never allow it to slow you down. I did not allow Asperger's syndrome to slow *me* down. I have personally delivered this message to hundreds of children all across Orange County. My hope is that I can now speak to thousands more.

"Do you have a photographic memory?!" is the common question that I get asked *all* the time.

Ugh! I moan to myself. There is not anything more annoying than to hear that question. However, I never blame anybody for thinking it. I may never know when people think that about me because they do not say it to me; they just assume without confirming it. The thing that nags me is when people automatically surmise that I have one, but I do not. Rest assured, I forget things *all* the time.

When people hear the truth but refuse to accept it, then that gets to me more. With Asperger's, whenever somebody does not believe me, it probably drives me up a wall ten times higher than the average person.

After floods of accusations, I proclaimed once and for all that "contrary to popular belief, I do not have a photographic memory." I said this during my required senior speech in English class for the Senior Exit Project. We all started laughing out loud. As of now and probably always, people just need to take my word for it. Unless I missed my guess, it is impossible for me and anyone to *disprove* having a photographic memory or any other skill for that matter.

Nevertheless, there is seemingly overwhelming evidence that I do not have such a memory. For instance, why would I be a century off on a game show that was going to air all throughout television and probably the internet? Furthermore, why would I be stuttering if I could simply read a mental snapshot as clear as day in my mind? If these are just misconceptions of having a photographic memory, then it further helps solidify my claim by proving that I do not have firsthand experience.

The real reason why I have the type of memory that I do have is because of Asperger's. It is not just facts but also personal history and dates as well. I remember before preschool—back at least to when I was two. Furthermore, I have found *patterns* in things. I could even take shapes, numbers, and mathematics, and employ them in the formation of mnemonics. I can write a short story just explaining how I memorized the president's birth and death dates alone.

Eventually, I had all the countries of the world memorized by 2012 and all the elements of the Periodic Table by July 2014. Again, it is merely patterns, associations, and other memory tricks. Yet, for people who are autistic, it appears to come easy for us intrinsically. Nevertheless, there are people who are not autistic who have a great memory too. I am not the only intelligent person. Moreover, I know for sure that I am not the smartest person in the world. There are countless people out there who are *far* smarter than me. I am not even striving to be the smartest.

Why do I memorize then? Why do I make sure that I am familiar with various subjects? Number one, it is easier to memorize, but I really do it to help children comprehend things in math, history, science, and more. I aspire to get into tutoring and ultimately become a teacher. My talents—like juggling, piano playing, card tricks, rope tricks, coin tricks, and other skills—is to receive the rewarding privilege of putting smiles and joy on people's faces.

In the end, I do not know where I would be had I not self-taught myself how to juggle. Through juggling and memorizing the presidents, I instantly got to know and befriend a myriad of people of all ages. Had I neither learned to juggle nor had the ability to find patterns in things and memorize, then I might never have connected with most of the people at my school.

People with autism and Asperger's (most, if not all) are innately shy. Therefore, my own timidity might have sequestered me from just about everyone. I am not "cured" of shyness in its entirety, but juggling and having things memorized are some elements that greatly helped me.

I am simply thankful beyond words that I was not mocked or attacked. In the movies and children's television shows that I grew up watching, *everybody* depreciated and condemned "smart" people. The writers parodied them by making them wear strange attire and talk in a nagging voice. To continue this burlesque slapstick rhetoric, the "smart" people seemed to be viewed as an outcast and beaten up. Personally, I had always gotten disturbed because of that. Some people can walk away from it and never think about it, but for me, I can probably walk away from it, but the perturbing images *cannot* escape my mind. I am still getting over some of the things that I watched when I was really young.

My prevailing theory is that those fictional characters had *boasted* about their intelligence; they superciliously made sure that their knowledge and/or skills were made known to everybody. That, I have reason to believe, is what set me apart. Plus, I do not dress or talk like them. Having Asperger's, I shiver at arrogance and loathe thinking about it.

I hate talking about myself in that manner, even if I am talking about my modesty. I cannot barge into a group of acquaintances and start saying, "Hey, look what I can do. Look what I know." (I am not saying that people without autism are like that either.) That was not how I was raised. I never inherited such a prideful quality of egocentrism.

> *And whosoever shall exalt himself shall be abased; and he that shall humble himself shall be exalted* (Matthew 23:12).

In fact, I have friends who knew me for months and even years before they found out what I could do and the things I know. One student teacher was reading about my knowledge of the presidents in the yearbook and started laughing in disbelief. Nearly gasping, he got out, "What? No way!" And we had known each other for months.

People know what I can do because others told them about me, because they read about me, or because I got to share one or two things about myself in class and in performances.

> *Let another man praise thee, and not thine own mouth; a stranger, and not thine own lips* (Proverbs 27:2).

God has been taking me to various places, and I am thankful. I am very grateful for the ability to juggle, which would probably not have happened had it not been for an airshow and an aunt who loves planes.

7

Habits and Worries

Day and night, some routines have become a tradition for me and will not let go of me. I always, always tried to hide them from everybody. For me, these habits are a burden—especially those cockamamie ones that cause difficult breathing.

At a young age, I became consciously aware that I was allowing habits to run my life. Some of them stuck because my mind tenaciously refused to let them go. They became worrisome so that I felt that something bad would happen if I did not do them.

An example, in my case, was double touching. Back around fourth grade, if I touched something with my right hand, for instance, like my chair or desk, then I felt compelled to touch it with my left hand, and vice versa. Likewise, I did it with my inner or outer right or left foot.

When I am walking, my ring and little finger might barely brush up against a fence. Consequently, I used to feel the need to turn around and touch the same spot of the fence with the same fingers on my other hand, with an equal amount of magnitude and velocity. If I kicked something like a soccer ball with my right foot, then I felt like I needed to kick it again with my left foot.

I do not know why. I used to feel unevenness if I didn't follow a habit. Then one day, I eventually got over it and essentially quit. The strength to overcome such a habit also stuck out to me in an admirable way.

Sure, it is understandable that I need to organize my backpack scrupulously and straighten out every single thing. I do it for concentration. Otherwise, it will intrusively linger in my mind while the teacher is talking, or while I am studying and reading independently.

"You can get over it," a person might say. "*I* would. No sweat."

"Well uh, I *know* I can…but *with* sweat," I'd reply.

Via strong perseverance, I quit several habits, but right afterward, new ones infiltrated in uninvited. For me, breaking habits is analogous to breaking tradition, as they sort of became a tradition. If I did not do them, then I would panic that I might feel panicked later on in regret. My mind kept telling me that it would only take me an extra couple of seconds to do them. Soon, I had daily routines; notice that the word "routines" is plural.

For example, all my pictures and posts on Facebook are painstakingly arranged, as I attempt to chronicle them the best I can.

Somewhere in my elementary-school years, I started a habit with staircases and stairwells. Whether going up or down, I felt like I always had to skip one step once, followed by two steps. Then one morning a couple of years later, I simply quit that habit. Ever since, I walk up the stairs normally. I only skip steps if I am in a hurry, but not because I feel like I *have* to.

In case you are wondering, I do *not* do elevators voluntarily unless I have a medical procedure on an upper floor and am weak. Other times, it may be something that happens once in a lifetime (sort of). On July 30, 2017, I took a round trip up and down the elevator of Wilshire Grand Center in Downtown Los

Angeles to the seventieth floor. However, I had to rest immediately after the fast ride down before my legs nearly collapsed on me. For a while afterward, I felt like I was still on the elevator, but it was totally worth it! The view overlooking Los Angeles and surrounding cities was spectacular! I was practically at eye-level with the nearby U.S. Bank Tower.

Having Asperger's syndrome, I view things much more precious than most other people. April 5, 2006, for example, was a special day. I watched on the news the night before that it would be 1-2-3-4-5-6 at 1:02:03 on 4/5/06. Well, that exact time (when it came around in the afternoon) was toward the middle of lunch. Back in fourth grade, I started volunteering to help out in the special day class during recess and lunch. That is where I went on this day. If I remember accurately, I looked up at the clock and may have missed it by seconds, but I figured out that it can still be 1-2-3-4-5-6 at 1:23 P.M. too. Since it was early-out Wednesday, that time was three minutes after the school bell, but my teacher allowed me to stay afterward.

Since then, I have dwelled on what would have happened if I missed it and have realized that ultimately nothing would have happened. It is supposed to be more for fun, but the stress never goes away. I remember 12:12:12 P.M. on 12/12/12; I was in the school library at Newport Harbor High, and I watched the second hand pass by.

When rare occurrences happen (like a special date and time, astronomical events, or a famous person comes to town), I want to be able to witness it and then share it with those who may want to hear about it. It sometimes makes me worried to think about what I should do when these dates arrive. Where should I go? Who should I tell?

Again, the culprit is Asperger's syndrome. It makes my mind tell me, "This story is just breaking," or "This date (or event) only happens once a decade," or "...once in a lifetime." For instance, on June 30, 2015, Jupiter and Venus were a third degree apart from each other in a planetary conjunction—the closest that they have been in two thousand years. Therefore, I was out taking pictures and looking through my telescope. (It was amazing, just to say.) March 14, 2015 was colloquially known as "The Ultimate Pi Day of the Century," and I wore a special T-shirt that said so.

Another unnecessary habit appeared in sixth grade. I made sure that at lunch, I sat at the same spot toward the right end on the same side of the same lunch table. Some days came with challenges by my fellow classmates who wanted to sit there, but my mind reminded me, "Come on, Matthew. You can do it for one year. You made it this far. Otherwise, you'll have to wait until seventh grade for your next chance." I had to politely ask if I could sit there, and they typically complied. Other days, I had to go toward the middle and ask people to move a bit over to their left. I did that all the way from left to right until the right end was unoccupied. Ultimately, I sat at the same spot every time. A lot of my friends and even the lunch aide had figured out my endeavor anyway.

Back in those years, due to having Asperger's syndrome, I wanted to try and do something for one year...at least. I felt compelled to do so. If I got something like a music box, for instance, my goal was to play it once every single day forever. In each of those cases, I foundered. It would unequivocally be a burden to try and find out how long I could go. What if I am on day 999 and missed day 1,000? I personally do not even want to think about that. Thus, it is best to take a deep breath and essentially let it go.

Whether it is habit or whether it is worry, I looked around at all my classmates. They neither have the same, strong grip to maintain habits as I do nor worry over things that I do. So why should I? While at Ensign Intermediate School one day, we heard a siren, and I worried that something happened at the house or maybe a car accident. My mind came up with all these hypothetical scenarios that were probably untrue. I panned the classroom and took notice that nobody else panicked. Plus, what are the chances that the siren was going to anybody that any of us knew, considering the population of the area?

I am still apprehensive when small, simple items are incredibly expensive. Certain meals cost over a thousand dollars. That is enough to make me lose my appetite, even upon thinking about it. What if it required days to prepare and the person is full at that particular hour of the day?

When I became conscious of the reality of choking or scalding hot water, I became unnecessarily prudent. Finally, I could not take it anymore. Whenever I ordered a hamburger back in the mid-2000s, I would have nearly everything *off* of it. I practically had a hamburger with just the condiments. Soon, one-by-one, I slowly added things back on.

In September 2006, a few weeks after sixth grade started, we learned about Adolf Hitler and the horrors of the concentration camps. I have heard and seen pictures of Hitler prior to this, but I never learned about the magnitude of the Holocaust before. My teacher talked about the terrifying details and showed us pictures. For simplicity, it was half audiobook and half teaching.

In my mind, I panicked. I went up to the teacher during the reading portion. I wanted to request if this could stop for the day, for I could not handle it any longer. I literally began having labored breathing. I kept imagining the hypothetical of my family going through this. I could not help but think of what would happen if we attempted to run away. I kept thinking about me and/or my family getting shot with nobody showing compassion for us.

I did not want my teacher to stop the CD, but she did. I did not want anybody else to know that I was having anxiety over this. Thus, I tried to whisper, but with my impediment and being shaken up over this, she could not understand me. I looked around, and everybody was staring at me. Embarrassed, I went back to my seat and tolerated it.

I am not joking, but I only ate lunch *all* week. *All* week. No breakfast. No dinner. I was incredibly scared at the terror that really happened to real people. I did not want to live through it. Finally, on that Friday, I made myself a couple pieces of toast; it was the first dinner that I had for days.

I am obsessed with cleanliness.

I always have hand sanitizers on me and at home. Even then, I always want to eat ordinary finger foods without using my hands. I do this approximately 99.9 percent of the time. I spent years of laboriously hiding it due to embarrassment and ridicule. This is mostly why I dislike eating in public, among a couple of other details. I just do not know what others will say, or how much they will tease me over it. Will I ever hear the end of it? Will they tell the world? Well, I still do not like eating in public, but I am no longer *too* ashamed to admit this.

I simply cannot fathom how people could eat with their hands in most circumstances. I have witnessed people eating what was on the floor, as well as eating after handshakes, touching coins, currency, or papers. I even saw a couple of my chemistry professors eating with their hands after touching pens, the overhead projector, their metal office key, and who knows what else. They or other chemists might have used those things at some point after handling reagents in a lab or a student's lab report without washing or sanitizing their hands.

I mean, I can probably write a novel articulating the things that I had witnessed ever since preschool. You can probably tell by now that it annoys me to see people carelessly picking food up with their hands and eating them. And guess what. They always seem to be fine. So why can't I eat with my hands or temporarily hold things with my mouth, such as a pencil, like other people? I think it only takes one moment for something irreparable to occur.

I eat formal-restaurant hamburgers, French fries, and other foods with a knife and fork. I eat fast-food hamburgers with the paper that it was wrapped in, as well as donuts and croissants. I eat not only sandwiches, but a lot of other things in sandwich baggies—including cereal, chips, pancakes, and desserts. As for granola bars or candy bars, I open the package slightly and slide it upward; that way, I eat it without touching it. Countless times, I had broken away and started using my hands, becoming confident, only to eventually regress back to it.

I usually take a pass when I am at an event, and somebody offers me a sample to eat if that sample requires me using my hands. If food is out in a buffet, I look around so nobody would notice me using a fork or napkin to pick it up. I usually take the second plate in the stack instead of the one on top. On top of that, it is intimidating for me to try and sneak a few bites of something while holding a napkin up to my face. I hardly touch my straw either. Furthermore, I make sure that there are neither any rips nor tears anywhere on the paper that the straw is wrapped in. I am always conscious of who may be staring at me during these entire, laborious procedures.

Nevertheless, I am not concerned with touching. I have given people handshakes and hugs. I have brushed up against walls, fences, and plants without any problem. I always hold the door open for people and use my hands to type, write, and flip pages in a book. Nothing like that bothers me.

It is hard to throw *anything* away because they are glued to dates and memories. Even little things can be attached to some memory—from pens to scraps of paper. All of my notes that I jotted down are dated and filed away (or piled away).

I cannot fathom how anyone can rip up and throw away their schoolwork since we work so long and hard to get good grades. I always kept the papers and drawings that I did. I have been keeping all my receipts since 2007. I have found genuine mint errors on some coins/currency in pocket change. However, some of the change evokes a special time in my life when I got them. Perhaps, I got them from a friend on the same day that I did something big.

This could moreover be applied to anything and not just pocket change. Do you want to take a guess, other than papers, pens, and pencils? Guess napkins. Guess party plates. Guess clothes. Guess my old backpacks and snack bags. Guess arbitrary things like that.

Yes, I sold stuff at yard sales and threw many things away, but I cannot stand the thought of regret and remorse over getting rid of what could be sentimental memorabilia. What if they remarkably become a collectible overnight? What if I permanently destroy something, sent it off to the dump, and felt contrite about it? In that case, that is it. It is gone for good. Nothing can ever bring it back, so I probably will never see it again.

I guess that I would feel detached. I might as well have thrown away a family picture, a working laptop, or a yearbook. Some of the ordinary shirts that I wore are attached to pictures. I remember several places where I was at while wearing those shirts. Thus, they have a big sentimentality for me.

Meanwhile, I simply stacked papers and other stuff off to the side. I pack the rest in bins and boxes. We place these receptacles away like in the closet or at storage.

With Asperger's, I cannot help all of this. A billion dollars could not change my mind.

In conclusion, I have constructed chains of thoughts in the past. The purpose is to replace bad, forlorn thoughts with good, outstanding ones. I used to fear that if I thought about something horrible from my imagination, television shows, stories, or movies—such as an amputation, other medical emergencies, explosions, a killing, wars, a wild animal attack, getting lost, being falsely accused and sent to prison—then it might happen.

Of course, that cannot happen. *Coincidences* happen.

As a real-life example, in seventh grade, I was really anxious that at any moment, the principal was going to speak through the intercom and say that there was a man with a gun or something. I had been meaning to tell somebody about this fear (like my mother, the principal, or R.S.P. teacher) to release the tension, but I kept neglecting to remember. Then on Tuesday, December 11, 2007, something similar happened. The principal said over the intercom, "This is not a drill." He had all of us go beneath our desks and had the teachers lock their doors.

It was my first lockdown, and it lasted for hours. Police and the bomb squad came, and we made it on the news. Apparently, a student brought what may have possibly been a small, homemade bomb. I even knew this person; he was in a couple of my classes.

Did I cause the lockdown to happen just by thinking it? Of course not, and it took a long while to realize that. There are hundreds of people at that school. How could I possibly determine what would happen just by thinking it, when there are so many minds thinking of various things. Several other people might be hiding the same fear and thinking about lockdowns constantly (or worse), yet it hardly happens if you really think about it. Importantly, several of my schoolmates did not let these things bother them.

I hypothesize that it is because I remember a lot of scenarios, especially things that I cannot get out of my mind and recall them at the most inopportune times. What I see in real life, on television, or in a movie can stand out to me. I am probably trying to remember these as life lessons so that I will not make the same mistakes.

When I used to immensely worry back in middle school, I would have taped on my binder Philippians 4:8. This Scripture verse directed me on the things that I should think about, rather than stressful, hypothetical scenarios. God does not want us to worry (Matthew 6:25 and Philippians 4:6), but to trust in Him.

> *For God hath not given us the spirit of fear; but of power, and of love, and of a sound mind* (2 Timothy 1:7).

In summary, certain habits are harder to get rid of than others, and they usually render worry and hypertensive stress. It is terribly easy for me to take a long time on small tasks, as I make sure that everything is in the right place.

Piece by piece, through taking deep breaths to counterattack the urge, I have broken and shattered several habits. They are often not done overnight. It just takes time and patience. I have done it before, so I know that I can do it again.

8

Organizing and Finishing What I Start

The tendencies to organize and finish what I start are a couple of the strongest, tenacious difficulties that many of us deal with.

It is not that I personally dislike organizing, it is that I cannot concentrate without it. Once I start, though, it is hard to stop. Added to this, I have to take my time. Everything (I mean *everything*) has to be in a certain order and in its right place, and I cannot relax until after it is done.

As I prepare for a classroom lecture or for homework, everything pertinent is stacked fastidiously and just off to the side. All my pens and/or pencils are lined up straight and facing toward the front. Everything else is neatly put away. All the loose papers are methodically collated together; others are in a specific folder or binder. I even would always square up the cards in board games just so that it would look neater. Back in my elementary school years, a friend with whom I played board games pointed it out to me. Until then, I must have not fully realized that I was doing it.

These are things that I felt like I *had* to do, yet had done some of them without thinking about it. At the thought of disorganization, I personally feel that I will be distracted. I might start organizing while the teacher or professor is lecturing. It is as nagging as cringes getting on my nerves. It is like the feeling when I rub my hands together, while hearing shoes scraping against cement, while fingernails scratch against the chalkboard, or while a washrag rubs on upholstery.

Those feelings rushed throughout my chest, abdomen, and arms while both typing out and later proofreading that last sentence. It is as if I am hearing these discordant, obnoxious cacophonies again live and in person. The very tips of my teeth begin to cringe and uncomfortably tingle.

Essentially, I cannot stand haphazardness—when all the books are not pushed the same distance inwardly on the shelf, when there is a glitch in the wall or floor patterning, when there is litter juxtaposing the cleanness of the grounds, when there is a typographical error, when my professor quickly erases the whiteboard and leaves some markings on it, or when a document does not have justified text.

Yes, I have since heard of what is known as Obsessive-Compulsive Disorder (OCD), and via firsthand experience, it is real! I alphabetize things, including my DVDs. Then, through habit, I attempted watching all of them in alphabetical order back around fifth and sixth grade, but I never completed that. Earlier, I was known to alphabetize the classroom library.

In third grade, during silent reading time, I would preoccupy myself with things other than reading, since reading is enervating for me. Reading never seems to go away. One day, I gathered all the A's and alphabetized them. Then the B's. Then the C's. Days later, when I was nearing the end of the alphabet, I noticed that several books were getting all out of order.

Today, I try and have most of my books together by category—for example, my Bibles and references, history, general sciences, medical sciences, anatomy and physiology, astronomy, atlases, encyclopedias, foreign languages, the literature books, and my puzzle books (like Sudoku, Fill-In, and various brain games). I could start my own library.

I have hundreds of books, if not a thousand, that still need to be placed in the right spot. Furthermore, all the books are inserted and fastidiously pushed into their bookshelves at the same distance, so I can smoothly run my finger along their spines. The valid reason of why they have not been properly placed in their own home yet is because once I start something, it is hard to stop.

It is certainly never just a hop, skip, and a jump. In fact, my mind reminds me of that. I attempt to do multi-day projects in one day. Furthermore, acquiring more stuff over the years protracts the time needed, creating a longer, tedious task. I had systematically spent hours at one time making sure that every square inch was orderly. I critically overthink where each book, pen, and piece of paper are placed. Simultaneously, I want to complete most of what I can in one sitting.

All of this is a direct consequence of my having Asperger's syndrome.

I strive to get all the laborious work out of the way first before going somewhere fun. Back when Pixar's *Cars* came out in 2006, I chose to spend a few hours cleaning and organizing under my bed first before going to the theaters. Unsurprisingly, I always like cleaning up around the room and organizing. When I was at the theater, I was incredibly thankful for my choice. Therefore, I got to relax there instead of dreading going home.

Additionally, I tend to finish whatever I started before going to sleep for the night to reduce the workload for the next day. Otherwise, I would just lie there for a couple of extra more hours than usual, organizing my thoughts on everything that has to be completed. It seems uncontrollable. I am always thinking, and my mind hardly gives me a break. It is honestly and utterly exasperating.

When I was in high school, I would always have extra stress when my grandfather or my mother found me still working in the middle of the night (even at the feeling that it was imminent). Somewhat humorously in retrospect, that further labored my breathing, increased my heart rate, and elevated my blood pressure by a few millimeters of mercury.

After I finally completed the work carefully, it usually takes a while just to clean up. That is a direct result from my thoroughness of having everything in its right place. I probably go to sleep a few seconds faster, knowing that everything is where it is supposed to be.

I always aspired to complete *every* game of chess and *every* game of monopoly. For chess, I used to not like draws or my opponent's resignation. One of my friends with whom I played chess a lot ended up having to mail me a photocopy of a glossary page from his chess book. There, he literally magnified the definition of the chess term "Resign" for me. As for Monopoly, I only got to complete the entire game a couple of times, relatively speaking. Several years ago, a couple friends of mine had the same zeal to finish a game of Monopoly as I had (and still have). One late night, we had to stop and finish in the morning—and that was the "Mega Edition."

Now, it is important for me to note that it is not just the tangible that I organize. Like sitting down to organize an essay, I organize my thoughts too. I list all my questions and comments in my mind before I say them—whether I am talking to a lifelong friend or raising my hand in class. I strongly dislike stuttering, but even after rehearsing, I can sometimes still stutter a little bit and forget what I was going to say. Nevertheless, it does help me to speedily articulate my thoughts and concerns while speaking.

9

My Zeal to Evangelize

I am an evangelist.

When I was really young, about nine or ten, I was called into ministry. Preachers prayed over me and got words from God, saying that I "have a calling into ministry," that I am a "young Billy Graham," and that I am "the next generational preacher."

I started evangelizing—which is telling others about Jesus and inviting them to church—with the children's ministry of California Victory Church. About once a month, I would go with the children's church and a few leaders into neighborhoods to evangelize. We generally went door to door, but sometimes, we went to parks or did an event in the community.

During one occasion, at Wakeham Park, another leader and I evangelized two ladies by the playground. Later on, when we were heading back, I saw those two ladies again and strongly felt that we should go back to them. I told the leader, and they ended up praying the Sinner's Prayer that day!

I loved evangelizing so much. We invited our children's pastor to come over to our house so that we could evangelize in my neighborhood. Every time we evangelized, we handed out tracts. We evangelized all over our neighborhood for years. What we started doing was planting and watering seeds in people's lives like in 1 Corinthians 3:6; according to the rest of that Scripture verse, God will give the increase.

In early 2007, along with five or six others from the children's church, I prepared for a humungous mission trip. By the middle of July, there were only three of us from the children's church remaining. We rehearsed nearly every Sunday after church. There were testimonies, puppet shows, and a skit from us. Finally, after months of rehearsing, preparation, and praying, the big day had arrived. It was five of us: our children's pastor, my mother who helped out, I, and the two others from the children's church who all carpooled together and drove to the Hesperia/Apple Valley area from Orange County.

Once we arrived, we started leaving invitation fliers on doors. We probably left hundreds of them (if not over a thousand) in various neighborhoods. At some point, one of the other two sat in the shade with both hands covering his entire face. As we drove down the boulevard, the children's pastor guessed the temperature. Shortly after, we looked outside at the big electronic sign that periodically rotated to the current temperature. To our wonderment, the children's pastor was right. Then again, she lived close by. It was ninety-eight degrees.

After cooling off at her house for a few hours, we went back out to more neighborhoods toward evening time. Before returning back to the house and rehearsing the entire event again, we went inside a store to quickly get a few things. It was there when I had my evangelistic zeal to pass out invitations to the people inside the store. So we did.

I hardly slept that night. The next morning we arose, got ready, and drove to the park.

One family. We had done the entire event, and only one family came. Nevertheless, it was a fun experience to be a part of the mission trip. All of us would do it again for even one person. Afterward, I said that it was quite probable that this family just happened to be there; they probably did not receive the invitation card. Our children's pastor thought that was amazing and felt that God perhaps had directed them there.

Toward sophomore year of high school, California Victory Church had a feeding-the-homeless ministry. Held every first Saturday of the month, a bunch of us arrived at the church very early in the morning, prayed together, and caravanned to the OC Civic Center at the crack of dawn. While some fed the homeless, several of us went out to evangelize. It lasted till 2011.

By senior year, I desired to evangelize my fellow schoolmates again. Now, I need to append that it is often intimidating, but I simply pray for courage. I also pray for the Holy Spirit to go before me and to speak through me. It is nevertheless better when I have a buddy to go with me. I evangelized intermittently at Newport Heights Elementary, Ensign Intermediate, and a little bit already at Newport Harbor High by this time.

There are Scripture verses that are encouraging to me when it comes to the fear of persecution, such as Romans 8:17, 1 Peter 3:14 and 4:16, as well as the following:

> *Blessed are ye, when men shall revile you, and persecute you, and shall say all manner of evil against you falsely, for my sake* (Matthew 5:11).

> *If we suffer, we shall also reign with Him: if we deny Him, He also will deny us* (2 Timothy 2:12).

> *Choosing rather to suffer affliction with the people of God, than to enjoy the pleasures of sin for a season* (Hebrews 11:25).

In junior year, I became a captain for FCA (Fellowship of Christian Athletes). In early 2013, my heart reminded me of *my zeal to evangelize.* I proposed to everybody in the leadership that we should go out and evangelize at our school together. I soon printed out the questions for the leadership team's review.

Finally, one early morning before school, we met by the Tommy Tar statue near Dodge Hall, evangelized, and invited people to come to FCA. A few of the other captains had gotten a couple boxes of donuts. Afterward, there were still more donuts left over; I believe that there were two boxes. Everybody was heading to class. The captains decided for a person to take a box and give the donuts away to their classmates.

Except me. I thought to myself, *No way!*

I later came up with an analogy that each one of those donuts represented a potential life who could have been saved that day. After I had spontaneously thought of that, I immediately offered to take one, but another captain wanted it. (I did not have a second period (which was the first class that day, so I ended up getting the box of leftover donuts by winning a game of Rock, Paper, Scissors. Thus, I got to invite a few more people. At least *all* of us got to plant and watered seeds that day.

Unfortunately, it was only once that we did that together.

In 2014, California Victory Church started evangelizing in neighborhoods once again—open for the congregation. There were usually just a few of us, including a few pastors. Alas, it only lasted a few months, but it was super fun as always.

10

The Struggles of Reading and Test Taking

"Once upo…Once upon a…a…time…"

A few seconds later.

"Once upon a time, there…"

Breathing.

"…there was…"

Matthew, this is going to take forever, says my mind.

"…there was a…Once upon a time, there was a…"

Matthew, you have this to do. You have that to do. You have to do this after that.

Something that I am quite abashed of is my relentless, exhausting, infamous, cockamamie struggle with reading. (The above was merely used as an example.)

Yes, I definitely struggle with reading, even though I love creative writing. I am constantly inundated with reading assignments, and there is not anything I can seemingly do about it. My mind persistently distracts me and diverts my attention by a thought or a noise. I can even get dizzy.

Contrastingly, I read all the time. In fact, I independently went through all five levels of *Hooked on Phonics* back when I was around four, five, and six. I enjoyed them so much that I went through them *multiple* times.

That oxymoron is as perplexing as the truth of having this notorious struggle to read. (Needless to say, I did *not* earn the Reading merit in Royal Rangers.)

Reading, through *my* eyes, could be full of tongue twisters. It is not necessarily what is *in* the text that is hard. I just always disliked it. Several questions that children and adults ask me are "How?" and "Why?" "What makes reading so difficult for you?"

Whenever I open up a book—even in the morning—it is as if I had stayed awake for sixteen hours doing homework. For as long as I could remember, reading is like a hundred pound weight of tiredness being pressed down on my head. The letters T-E-X-T put together in that sequence makes me drowsy. It is as if I took a nighttime medication for a cold. I imagine these heavy books being filled with words, page after page after page after page…with no pictures!

Reading is a humungous factor of why homework always kept me up till ten and eleven o'clock at night—at least—all throughout high school and college. Sometimes it was midnight and later when I finally got to bed.

I enjoy acid-base titrations in Chemistry lab. It is analytical. It is *precise*. There are special procedures to be done in a specific order. You have to make some of your calculations to the ten-thousandths place. (That is just perfect for a person like me who has Asperger's syndrome). However, I have firsthand experience of how frustrating it can get. With an acid and phenolphthalein in the Erlenmeyer flask, a half of drop of base from the graduated burette can be too much. Then you have to back-titrate. Parallel that frustration to my struggle with reading!

When I read, my mind may not stop talking. The gramophone in my brain reverberates music or dialogues constantly. One or two words can evoke a conversation I had or several loud choruses of a song. I could start being preoccupied over things that I have to do and how time is running out (even when I have a long time left to read). Pretty soon, and more often than not, it could take a stressful minute just to rock climb over a short sentence.

Imagine trying to fall asleep when you are completely awake. Your mind will not stop talking. It is reviewing obligations that you need to attend to or practicing on what to say to people in certain situations. You might as well try going to sleep in the middle of the day or at night with loud music playing in your ears. It is akin to trying to concentrate with reading when the volume is turned all the way up on the T.V. set or radio.

I mean, does my mind think that it has a mind of its own or something? Come on, for crying out loud! From about third grade until now, I *really* tried hard in learning to like reading, but pretty soon, I seemed to founder. I could not fathom how *anybody* could enjoy reading.

In fifth grade, distracted by the relative quietude of the room, I looked up at my fellow classmates. Silently and unsmiling, they all had their books open at an arm's length away and stared at the page. In their minds, they were probably enjoying the storyline. Reading is essential, though, but I still looked at those chapter books in awe.

In the summer of 2007, a bank teller gave me helpful advice, such as reading ten pages a day.

Here is my analogy though: if readers can read, let us say, at the speed of sixty pages an hour, then I could read at five to ten pages an hour. It is egregious!

I will never forget a time in junior year when there was a book that we had to read. I guess I could not get the audiobook to listen and follow along like I often got to do. It was Memorial Day weekend 2012, and I was spending late hours struggling to finish reading. It was not even due the next day, but I wanted to get the most done (at least half) that I possibly could. That way, I would have less to read the next day. Well, on this night, my grandfather came in. He asked me what I was doing or if I was going to bed soon. After all, it was like two o'clock in the morning!

The way reading assignments have been assigned to us was under the assumption that *everybody* can read flawlessly without a laborious struggle. The teacher might as well have said to me, "Here is the book you can borrow. Take your time, but I need it back in ten minutes." Shaking, I would look down at the book, then slowly back up at the teacher, and reply, "But this is 1,000 pages." Yet the teacher, bewildered, says, "Yeah? So? What's the problem?" (This, of course, was for illustration purposes, but closely parallels reality for a lot of us).

Back in fourth grade, I enjoyed reading those short books about real people and places instead, but later on, I attempted chapter books once again. The *Goosebumps* series was very popular, so I started reading one…again. It was #33 entitled *The Horror at Camp Jellyjam*. I later started alternating chapters between this book and *Sideways Stories from Wayside School.* Pretty soon, I got lost in the reading. In fact, it was fun. I ended up finishing both books around the same time, and truthfully, I felt such a rewarding feeling inside. Thus, in fourth grade, my reading started to improve.

Over the next couple of years, I read all three *Wayside School* books twice, as well as a total of fourteen *Goosebumps* books. I did try other books, but I had to stop.

I feel equally jubilant when I get closer to the end of a book and flip through all the pages that I have read with a sense of pride and accomplishment. Before eighth grade, all of us had to read Carl Hiaasen's *Hoot.* I *flew* through that chapter book. I think I read forty to fifty pages in one day.

This is the answer that I found: I do read better when it is something that I am interested in and something that I *want* to read and know about. As I grew older, I was mainly interested in history and various science (i.e., nonfiction). Nonetheless, I do *much* better when I listen to audiobooks or watch videos and animations. I also read better if I am reading out loud in front of people.

Since I am a kinesthetic learner, I need movement to concentrate, such as tapping. Likewise, I used to resort to pacing around the house while simultaneously holding my book or textbook and reading. While I am a passenger in a moving vehicle, reading seems to improve more because of the higher speed.

On December 13, 2008, I was at a Trinity Broadcasting Network (TBN) studio. It was the final rehearsal of a Christmas program that I was in for the next day, but it never aired on television for some reason. During rehearsal, I saw a small girl up on stage reading the Bible. She looked like she was really concentrating on what she was reading. I will never forget it. That moment right then and there *inspired* me to start reading from Genesis 1:1 come January 1st.

I became excited to find out what some of the books that I had never read before were all about. I became excited to read for myself the Bible stories that I was taught. On January 1, 2009, I started reading the Bible from Genesis at my own pace. I read at least three verses a day. Here and there, I read a chapter or few.

Again, my mind cannot stop talking. Other people can control it, but I apparently cannot even though I employ perseverance. Reading almost every single day and praying before each time I read, I completed the Old Testament on June 30, 2016 (seven and a half years since I started). Even though many people could read the entire Bible in a year or less, I still feel quite accomplished and became excited to start the New Testament. Each Bible book in the Old Testament now evokes the memory of where I was and what I was doing at or around that time of my life while reading it.

I am super eager to learn. It is my zeal, which is why I have a huge library at home filled with reference-like books. I like the elating feelings of taking a physical book (like a history, mathematics, or science book) out and studying in it. However, when I go to look up one thing (or even on the internet), I could spend hours learning. To the point of exasperation, one thing can cause me to look up another, and then another. A chain reaction is thus born.

Personally, I much prefer nonfiction over literature, because I desire to know things that could be applicable to everyday life. I also want to understand *everything* that I read and be able to retain the littlest of detail. Well, I acknowledged how it is impossible to know everything, so I try and do as much as I physically can. That way, I could be best prepared for if and when a person asks me about anything, for I still have a strong passion to become a teacher.

So why has it been easy for me to fall behind on the reading for my favorite college courses? I understood a lot of the material and have mostly gotten A's and B's, but there are so many things packed in one chapter in a college book. It is a challenge to read every single page (even skimming through it). The faster the skimming, the lesser the retention is. In the summer of 2016, I decided to get some of my textbooks early to start studying, which is, of course, the best thing to do. (However, I still contend that *every single* textbook published should be put in audio format. Alright. That is unlikely.)

One day, I had to talk to one of my chemistry professors in her office. She was quite nice, helpful, and encouraging. I do not know how, but she simply discerned that I was trying to understand everything in the reading and lecture. It was amazing, for we only knew each other for probably a month at this point. She reassured me by saying that *she* herself still does not know everything there is to know about chemistry, and she is quite experienced in the field. She told me that she is still learning to this day.

Since I am quite talkative and enjoy conversations, I *always* have a list of questions ready for anyone knowledgeable about nearly any subject, such as a reverend, a firefighter, a chemist, a biologist, an astrophysicist, a meteorologist, a nutritionist, a doctor, a mathematician, an airline pilot, a mechanic, a historian, and a musician. I am always curious about how and why things work—in all the various sciences, mathematics, history, American Government, and so forth.

However, when I finally get the chance, my mind usually goes blank. It does not matter how much I rehearsed it beforehand. If I start to ask, I may stutter.

Of course, socially, I could still get nervous to ask. A lot of professionals *seem* busy and want to dodge any social contact from everybody; they seem to be in a rush. Of course, my Asperger's is telling me that.

Unsurprisingly, in high school, English seemed to have always been the longest class, even though it was the same amount of time as all my other classes. It was classes like Spanish, anatomy, algebra, and history that seemed to fly by fast. Now *those* are the relatively easy courses, whereas English is analogous to something like rocket science or quantum physics.

That is exactly how it is like for me. Everybody has different aspirations on who they want to be in life. People sometimes cannot understand how reading is a struggle for individuals like me. That is because reading comes so easy for them; they do not know what it is like to struggle with reading. However, I find algebra and trigonometry to be a piece of cake, and that can, therefore, lead me to the similar assumption that it should be easy for everybody.

What is easy for us who have autism could be hard for others and vice versa.

Quite similarly, I *have* to have extra time with quizzes and tests. Therefore, because I have Asperger's, I always had test accommodations. Most of the time, when I did not take advantage of the accommodations, I was the last person in class finishing up a test. I aspire to get every question correctly—every single one of them. That is my tenacious goal. Before every quiz and test, my mother and I would usually pray for remembrance and a clear, focused mind.

What do quizzes and tests require? Reading! Everyone has to *read* every question and every answer. I may *know* the material, but it still takes longer for me. If I *really* know the material, then I could finish rather quickly. Sometimes, we have to read the questions and answers carefully. In the back of my mind, I am always alert and prepared for trick questions, which *are* out there. Therefore, I accordingly take extra time thoroughly reading each word.

Nonetheless, music usually blasts through my head. It is worse when the same two seconds of a song reverberates over and over again and gets stuck. In reality, music helps me now and again. Because I am a kinesthetic learner and know how to play piano, tapping to the beat, or the thought of kinesthetically playing a part of the song on the piano, helps me to concentrate.

Then, when I think of or listen to the song at a future date, it may evoke the joys and excitements of taking that quiz or test.

Inescapably, I had gotten pressured more often than not when one-by-one, my classmates would go over to turn in their completed exams. My heart rate elevated even more when I was the last person, and my teacher was hurrying me up, saying that he or she wanted to get out of there.

"What number are you on, Matthew?"

Um, no comment. Alright, I had to answer. "Well, uh, I tend to skip around." As much as I endeavor to go in order, my peripheral vision makes out all the shorter questions scattered throughout the page. I consequently get those relatively easy ones out of the way.

I suppose reading is just a skill. The more I practice and persevere as I did with piano and juggling, the better it shall become. To this day, I believe that I have stabilized this struggle with all of the abovementioned improvements. However, because I have Asperger's, I still have a gigantic lingering residue of this struggle.

I have accepted that reading is just one of those things like skateboarding (a skill that I never got the hang of), inasmuch that I probably cannot take a book, sit down, and easily read it from cover to cover. Even thinking about that exhausts me.

I learned to compromise and accept this limitation that I personally have, but no matter how much it takes, and with patience as the key, I *still* aspire to get college degrees and do the big things that I want to do in life.

11

Creative Writing

Ever since Paularino Elementary School, I have given my teachers a lesson when it came to me and creative writing. Once I am given a prompt to write about, granted that I can use my imagination entirely, they need to expect a novella from me. Well…practically.

I inherently love creative writing. It is cathartic and is one of my several passions. So it is probably an oxymoron that I cannot stand reading.

With a stack of lined paper and a writing implement of some sort, I can create any story that comes to mind. It is just like art. With blank sheets of paper or a sketchpad, I can go anywhere on earth or in the universe.

My teachers quickly caught on about second grade. I remember being in the class that I started going to part time to test whether or not I was ready to be mainstreamed. That teacher had to tell me, "Don't go beyond this page." Soon after, I started writing small. I was able to fit a few extra lines into one. However, I knew too well that I could not fit it all in. Perseverant to write everything, I attempted to turn the page surreptitiously. By that time, the student sitting next to me had to take my pencil away! It was simply discipline.

Around that same year, in my regular class, I turned in a rough draft that was pages long. My teacher had to review it in front of me. I went over to a crescent-shaped desk for the evaluation. Using a red ink pen, she corrected the parts of my creative-writing essay that did not work well. The shattering part was seeing her put a red line through several of my sentences, saying that it was not necessary to use them.

Nevertheless, I still love to write and utilize imaginative ideas. Even at home, starting about third grade, I was creating stories and movie scripts on the computer for fun. I did my own illustrations too. Each of them was intended to be published. Alas, I never went through with any of them. Some ideas came from me, while others were inspired by a conglomeration of books, television shows, and movies. One-page assignments can easily turn into five pages. My mind simply cannot stop giving me ideas.

I overfill my stories with a plethora of details, as well as hidden codes and meanings even. Some codes could be symbolic, such as the naming of the characters and the time at which a clock or watch read. I always enjoyed coming up with the names of my characters and the places where they lived.

Like I previously said, creative writing is cathartic, a release of stresses. It has always been one of my favorite pastimes. Nowadays, I may jot down a few words of an idea for a book, college essay, or speech, but right toward the beginning, as I begin writing the simple idea down, words just simply flow out of my hand.

It fills me with a sense of belonging as if this is what I am going to be one day: a highly respected author…as well as a movie actor. (Again, I have written movie and television scripts also.) I love acting, but the hardest part was keeping a straight face sometimes. Friends at Newport Heights Elementary encouraged me to pursue acting after I pretended to lose consciousness a number of times.

I had acted in a couple of plays in 2006 and had a part in

the annual Newport Harbor High School movie; their movies were shown at the Lido Theater in Newport Beach. I further enjoy being a hidden-audience actor, which happened once at a first aid-CPR class in March 2013 at St. Andrew's Presbyterian.

Day and night, I am *always* critically thinking and cannot stop. I think as I try hard to fall asleep. I think while walking or even standing still. I think about new ideas and what I just learned, for example. I surmise that writing helps me to get my thoughts down and organized.

In tenth grade World History and Geography class during the fall of 2010, our teacher assigned a project to write about the French Revolution either as a storybook or an allegory. In this first-person story, which I titled *The Revolutionary Time Machine*, two kids procrastinated on the same project that I was just assigned. They found a secret computer, typed in a few codes that I made very specific, and were transported back in time to the French Revolution.

I must have spent tens of extra hours writing this short story and additional hours drawing most of the illustrations. Sometime after I turned in the story with over twenty pages, my teacher said that it was the best one that he ever read. "By far," he appended. The project got one-hundred percent.

To reiterate, I *always* desired with all my heart to publish several successful series of books. Now, it returned...again. I thought that I could use the same characters and computer to create more educational short stories about going back in time to learn and witness history.

In my mandatory four years of English at Newport Harbor High, I would periodically hand in between five and ten pages, even if it was not a creative writing assignment. Whether it was choosing a diagram to draw in a science class or needing to select from a list of prompts, I strived to choose the hardest one. If I had to choose one from a list of several, then I would settle on a few of them and smoothly blend them all together.

One of the enormous culminations to my creative writing skills came toward the end of that same year. This is the big one where I went overboard to the max!

My English teacher assigned a creative writing project in the spring of 2011. We had to take a real event that happened in our lives and fictionalize it. Furthermore, it had to be a *couple* of pages, but you cannot say that to me when it comes to creative writing.

I opened up a blank document on Microsoft Word. Soon I got *lost* in it. It was just me and the computer. It was as if I were secluded in a forest. My mind kept giving me more ideas, and I kept typing and typing. Closing it out and needing to go to sleep for the night became analogous to traveling a hundred miles back home. I could not wait to open it again and type some more. This is a direct consequence of my strong, tenacious pull to finish what I start.

Finally, after staying up late night after night after night, it was time to turn it in. Since I did not have a printer at home, I had to print it out in the morning.

"Can I go to the library to print out my story?" I requested in R.S.P. class. It was the first class of the day, followed by English. (I had the same R.S.P. teacher for all four years.) I said, "Guess how many pages it is."

"How many?" my R.S.P. teacher asked.

"Thirty-two," I replied and heard a nearby student gasp.

"No, *really*, Matt. How many?"

"I'm serious. Thirty-two." Right then and there, I realized that I should not have told her. I should have just gone over to the library instead. Panicked, I laughed and motioned to the hall pass by the door, saying something like "I-I'll just uh, go print it out if that's okay."

My teacher allowed me, and I rushed over there very quickly. I feared that…I do not know what. Perhaps she would not have allowed me to print it out. When I came back and showed her my over eight thousand word story of thirty-two pages, she almost did cartwheels and somersaults.

Now it came time to go to English class. I hid my essay so that no one would say anything. I just did not want my teacher to know just yet. Alas, after class started, our teacher had everyone hold their stories up. I shyly held up my thirty-two pages. One of my friends chuckled in awe, wide-eyed, which initiated a chain reaction of chatter.

A couple of weeks later were the finals. As always, my English final probably took the longest. I sat there in my R.S.P. room for *hours* and *hours* finishing up that huge final! My English teacher actually came in a couple of times, and I was the only student there. He eventually told me with a huge apology that he did not have time to read my entire paper but gave me an A.

That summer, I got the opportunity to read the thirty-two pages to my mother and Ginny Carr in Fullerton. Being a coauthor with her late husband herself, she verbally critiqued it. She said parts were too long and that I need to watch out for that, but overall she liked it. She gave me the idea to go to the library and find out if I could enter my story, or at least part of it, in a contest or something. Perhaps I could publish it.

At the library, I found out about the 2011 contest of creative writing, which is an annual summer competition eligible for high schoolers. One guideline required that it had to be a maximum of 2,500 words. The winner will get published in their magazine and given $250.

I went home and took that thirty-two-page paper and spent weeks cutting it down like a tree trimmer. I went through it over and over and over again until it was just under 2,500 words. As it turned out, I did not win, but that did not stop me. I wrote an entirely new story for the summer of 2012. I did not win that year either, but I was satisfied with trying. And that is the best anyone can do: just try your best and have fun. I have already learned to accept that.

Lastly, in freshman year, during the fall of 2009, I tried equally as hard on a script for a short play. In my drama class, a guest speaker came by to give us a unique opportunity. The project was to write a short script, and the winner would have their play performed, get paid $250, go to Los Angeles, and actually cast their own characters.

After his introduction, we all started on a script. Afterward, finished or not, a couple of us got to have our scripts acted out. I volunteered mine to be one of them. From my fellow classmates who volunteered to act it out, I got to cast my own characters. It was amazing to hear my words being acted out by other people.

Afterward, the guest complimented me. To the entire class, he pointed out one tiny but impactful part that I had done exceptionally well on, so I decided to enter the competition. At least once, I stayed up late at night working on it. (Again, I tend to finish what I start). Ultimately, another classmate won, who was a friend of mine, but I will never forget the fun I had with the project.

My main message is that anybody can do the best they can, but they should also have enjoyment while doing it. The more you set time to put in the work, the higher the grade you'll get. When it comes to competitions, writing (or anything) should be cathartic instead of competitiveness in the long run. The more people who enter a race, sure, the more competition, but there is still a chance. Regardless, creative writing should be serene and a place to escape, as it is for me.

12

Shyness and Social Interactions

Sometimes, I seem to live vicariously with people who are completely friendless, and that bothers me. I *empathize* with them. I *know* what they are feeling. I *understand* all the hurting inside. I feel those feelings myself. I start to feel selfish.

Thus, if I spend time with friends and not *them* (unbeknownst to me that they live in such pain), then they may look at me and think that *I* am one of those people who ignore them. Likewise, I loathe the thought that people could be envious of me. I hate that. That could render me shy as well.

This short story is a tad lengthier, as it articulates one of the *hugest* characteristics of autism.

When I approach people or vice versa, or when I am walking opposite a vehicle on the sidewalk, my head is usually down, looking at my watch or cell phone. Other times, when I look at houses or trees, my head is quivering and my eyes are shaking, darting back and forth, and up and down. It is as if I am viewing the world through the rapid-moving slits of a zoetrope, or old film in the early motion pictures. I do not know who is staring at me or not.

Do I look normal or crazy to them? I wonder.

These may not even be going through their minds, but I am

prudent not to hurt anybody else's feelings. I usually look up at them shyly at the last second. Suddenly, in a flash of lightning, it is over, and they passed by. It only lasted a couple of seconds, but it seemed like minutes.

Since I was born with Asperger's syndrome, I was born with diffidence. When I was really young, I would feel embarrassed over nothing and hide behind my mother. Throughout school, I was magnetically held back from peers by this "Block of Nervousness" as I call it.

I have always seemed to be nervous while going up to people—even best friends. I feel like the person at an event who has to ask for money or donations from everybody. Asking to spend time with anybody or talking in class could equate to costing a million dollars. On the other hand, I love speaking in class. I am characteristically eager to explain something that I know, but my professors often explain everything without first asking the class if anybody knows it. However, I ask myself, "What if I'm totally wrong and people laugh?" or "What if people disagree with my opinions and chastise me over this one thing?"

I gain this extra nervousness by the shows I watched, personal experience, and the things that I have witnessed. I tried not to be like the characters on those kids shows who always made mistakes. I endeavored not to make the mistakes that I made before that caused my fellow classmates to be mad at me. I used to be greatly competitive in almost anything: board games, sport, class projects, and so on.

At Newport Heights Elementary, I became notorious when it came to handball. I just did not like having to stand in line and wait for my next turn. I was impetuous.

However, discipline helped me to improve in sportsmanship and manners. Seeing how people reacted when I would lessen their playtime or be a distraction during class further helped me learn how to be more polite. Discipline shaped me into who I am today; I learned from my past mistakes. I became prudent in my choices and may be unrecognizable to the person I once was.

Nevertheless, I sometimes did not have to do anything. There have been several people who disparagingly came after me just because I was different. They would belittle me just because I talked and acted differently. They would depreciate me just because I was reticent. People would deride me and tell me to go away. They would pretend to do a lot worse than beat me with innuendos. I am just thankful that I was never in a fight. Sometimes, they just intimidated me because they wanted to see me cower and have somebody to laugh at. Alas, the reality is that some children *do* go through much worse. Bullying should thus be eradicated, but that cannot easily happen. In the interim, people should continue the fight in stopping it as they have been.

Most people with autism and Asperger's are much more sensitive and defensive than others. A little, harmless tease or when a friend does not believe our word can equate to the feeling of being bullied. We may worry if they are mad at us, or if they are reconsidering our friendship.

I am not dwelling on these things because it is not just me. I am empathetic toward others. I should not feel egotistical or be mad because some people treated me differently. I feel sorry for all those who were teased and even bullied a hundred times more or ten times less than me. I know how it feels. I have hundreds of friends, but some people may only have one or two.

People need to understand that teasing and bullying lead to frustration, which leads to anger, which leads to irrational acts of violence. People became prejudiced and leaders like Malcolm X came along. Opposite that leader was the peaceful leader, Rev.

Dr. Martin Luther King Jr. who opposed violence. (Both Malcolm X and Dr. King Jr. were assassinated, but they both had a similar mission toward racial equality.) It is the question of both method and right-versus-wrong.

This all may not thoroughly explain my innate shyness. When I go up to people, I feel as if a magnet is repelling me back. The greater the number of people, the stronger the force. It is a direct proportionality. When I talk out loud in a classroom or with other people, my impediment has *always* gotten in the way. I wonder if I am interrupting my friends. I ponder whether or not I am being intrusive. Will I say anything that will make them think that I am strange…or stranger? Are they annoyed with me?

I personally cannot stand the times when people give me a hard time and then laugh so loud about it because they think that I really fell for it. The high volume of their insolent laughter hurts my ears. Sometimes, I do not understand other people's humor and do not know what to say at times like that.

What was it like when I was in preschool? Inside our classroom was a designated place to play. From what I remember, I would wander around, probably thinking, to find something to do. Many of my fellow classmates would play with miniature dinosaurs, but I do not recall being interested in playing with dinosaurs initially.

A main factor as to why I became bashful is that I am simply uninterested in several things that most people my age found entertaining, such as music, television shows, dancing, acts in talent shows, certain games, and even sports. I was neither interested in famous superheroes or action figures like most of my friends, nor listened to music like *Kidz Bop*. (As a small side note, I can say that I am old enough to remember when the first *Kidz Bop* came out; I remember watching the commercial.)

When I went to high school, I started getting more and more into dancing and music. The high school youth group would host such events. I still felt like I was awkward and backed away against the wall at times, but toward the end, I started getting closer toward the center.

It is like swimming. Sometimes you just have to dive in and start, while forgetting what people might be thinking of you and how cold the pool might be.

Furthermore, I did not understand the contemporary slang, onomatopoeias, or salutatory gestures immediately. I seemed to be the last person who was told about them. More precisely, I had to figure a lot of things out on my own.

When I got into kindergarten, my teacher told us emphatically, "We are *all* friends." However, not *everybody* obeyed that classroom policy. I recall walking by the swing set one day, and two of my classmates just yelled at me in such malevolent spite. They were scolding me, "Go away, Matthew! You're *not* our friend!"

Another day, I tried to play with my classmates out on the field, and the leader of them all called out to me, "You're not playing with us!"

Now, I *know* that I am intrinsically unsociable, *yet* every forlorn hardship that I had ever endured in my early childhood has always influenced how I approach people.

When I was in rehearsals for a play in 2006, we played an improv game called "Taxi." I hated the first time I played it. I waited in a long line, and every time I finally got inside the pretend taxi, the driver seemingly always chose me to get out after five seconds.

I used to have a couple of neighbors my age who almost always voted me out from their presence. I did not even do anything. It was solely because of who I am with Asperger's, I could be sure. (They were nice to me off and on.) That created another trial for me. People who teased me when we were younger, instantaneously became a great friend to me later. Then, I would feel guilty about being mad over what they had done. It felt immature to have gotten upset over it. Yet, there were inexcusable things that they did to me before we became better friends.

It was not always hard to be around peers or engage in a conversation, so I was never *totally* sequestered away from social contact. For some of us, it is easy; and for others, it is hard. It depends on the individual. I might be in between. As a child, I made a goal to make at least one new friend at our local McDonald's PlayPlace on Harbor Blvd. Most of the time, I met that goal.

As I grew older, things almost totally changed. I made many more friends. By the time I graduated from Ensign Intermediate School, I had made over a hundred who were my age, such as at school, church, and Royal Rangers.

Nearly all of them liked me for who I am. They liked my knowledge for the presidents, my juggling, my smile, my sense of humor, and just talking with me. I did not cuss, cheat, lie, or childishly fight. However, I was peer pressured with difficult situations to engage in surreptitious things a number of times, but since I remembered life lessons from how I was raised and from stories (either fiction or nonfiction), I simply did not want to suffer any repercussions. I knew that there would be consequences to follow regardless; if I was not caught, I knew I would feel guilt.

After special activities/events hosted by churches, schools, or friends, I became super ecstatic to participate. But every time it is over, everybody goes home. *I* have to start getting ready to go home. Soon after the end of the event, the joyousness fades away, and loneliness returns, but the memory never wears off. I still have those good memories permanently stored in my mind, but it is hard to bear when they are over. I wish time could move backward. The place almost seems empty and forlorn when there are only a few people left who are talking to one another. It begins to look different than it did a few minutes prior. It is as if it never happened. At home, I always am wondering when the next special activity is going to be—whatever it is and whoever hosts it.

These events are one of the rare times when I finally get to really socialize. Then, those feelings morph into additional forlorn pangs of nostalgia. Nostalgia is usually a warm feeling, but sometimes, things are too sentimental and evoke loneliness. Furthermore, it usually happens once an event is over.

Occasionally, I feel nostalgic when I listen to music (especially from a cello, violin, or organ). Likewise, when I smell an aroma; taste a meal, drink, or dessert; or hear old nursery rhymes.

When looking at all the black-and-white photos in my yearbooks from Paularino and Newport Heights Elementary, I contemplate on how my friends in those pictures and everybody else are all practically grown up by now. We are no longer kids.

Here is my Goliath-sized predicament, which leads to a giant state of quandary: I have had many, many, many fun times with friends and family, and I feel super thankful for having them. I would not trade or substitute them for anything else. Had I hung out with friends my own age a thousand times more than I did, a bunch of memories that I made may not have ever happened. They are like pros and cons. Nevertheless, I desire to socialize, even though it is hard for me.

I have had many dreams where I finally socialize, or was about to, but my friends never came, or I woke up. When I wake up, I realize that it was merely some forlorn dream in disguise. It deeply saddens me. I long to hang out with others but now am tied with sorrow. After these types of dreams occur every now and then, the somberness simply gets *worse*. The joy of spending time and talking with others leaves me all at once like a rush of wind or a mighty current in the river. At least the memories will always evoke the fun times that I *did* spend with friends.

I feel the same lonely feelings when seeing pictures of a group of children and the camaraderie among them, such as children with an arm around their friend, children standing up for bashful ones in the midst of bullying, children hanging out with each other, children singing, dancing, and having fun. Sometimes, I panic and have a hard time breathing when certain music or shows come on.

Here is another paradox: when I was roughly twelve, I sometimes watched a new show or a new movie before going to sleep for the night. I would enjoy them. A couple of them were mainly filled with child actors or child voice actors. Thus, there were friendships, helping each other out, adventures, and such. Strangely, I would wake up the next morning with a bewildering, forlorn sensation. I cannot entirely explain it. I completely felt deprived of friends and adventure. (I am not using the word "adventure" as in treasure hunts or anything. Rather, just simply hanging out. That is adventure. That is creating a memory.)

I did not want to watch what I just watched ever again, or at least for a long time. Even as far back as fifth grade, I desired to go back in time and start over. Not only would I remake friends, but I would be less nervous. I would be bolder. I would spend time with them more. I would sleep better. I would read and do homework better.

After elementary school, I practically never spent time with anybody from school during summer vacation. I usually stayed home, went on errands, visited family and family friends, and helped out my grandfather with tile setting. Up until now, people may not have ever guessed that I lived this way. I suppose that I endeavored to hide it. It makes me nervous to go forward and admit my struggle to anybody.

I am better at socializing and holding conversations today. I have improved in getting over shyness. I guess I feel guilty if I complain about it. I have received incalculable compliments all my life. One friend complimented me by saying, "If I could, I would be you for a day." Whether in school or out of school, several of my friends call out, "Hi, Matthew!" all the time. Then that is usually it. Sometimes, it leads to a conversation for a moment or two. What happens in between?

Most of the time at church, school, around the neighborhood, and other places, I get the opportunity to talk to a few people; but once I am at home, I usually do homework, projects, read, watch television, and am distant from any friends. Furthermore, homework keeps me up late at night. I also spent extra time with the details on specific projects. I do feel that I have been deprived of time to socialize because of this and my struggle to read. However, when I did have spare time, I used it to practice music and juggling, as well as doing art and film projects and such.

I have memorized the facts about the presidents. But how? How did I have *time* for all of that? By not socializing as much as I should have. Truth be told, I do not think I realized what spending time with peers was until intermediate school. Then, it hit me all of a sudden. I would spend time with family, friends from church, and neighbors, but they were all older, although I still enjoyed the great times nonetheless.

As time went on, I began stressing over it. The countdown to high school graduation became smaller and smaller. I became aware that I am greatly introverted when it comes to going up to people. I once struggled to ask a friend if he and his brother wanted to go to the movies while we were in eighth grade. He said sure, and we tentatively planned for Saturday, but it never happened.

I have gotten quite a few requests to hang out with others outside of school, but my shyness refused to allow me to go. My mind reminded me of homework, projects, books to write, and drawings to draw. It *is* easier when people ask me to hang out with them, but sometimes, my Asperger's declines their offer. I hardly could speak to anyone unless they invited me over to talk with them. By junior year, thankfully I started improving and began going up to my peers at school again.

A comical story was when I tried calling about four or five friends during a week off at school. I was tremendously nervous. It took at least ten or twenty minutes per person before I had the courage to press the call button. I only got parents and answering machines that day, so I never really got to spend time with peers that week. At least I tried.

In Spanish 1 class that same academic year, I kept giving hints to everybody. A few of us at a time had to write a sentence on the board in front of everybody while utilizing the new vocabulary terms. I would write a few times something like, "Yo paso al rato con nadie, porque yo estoy muy nervioso. Yo quiero pasar al rato con mis amigos un día," which literally translates to, "I spend time with nobody because I am very nervous. I want to spend time with my friends someday."

At places with a lot of people, I am like an invisible person. My eyes dart back and forth. and I might be sauntering, then abruptly turn around, not being able to decide where to go. I feel like I am turning 360 degrees, and everything else is spinning around me faster in the opposite direction. It could be tantamount to a suspenseful scene in a mystery movie. People rush past me in all directions. I usually lean against the wall because nervousness is holding me back.

I witnessed people jumping into a group all the time. Nobody else gets mad, so why should they get mad if I finally decide to do that? Still, I cannot seem to put one foot in front of the other, always worrying if I was intruding.

Truthfully, for years, I have been around people in high school, at youth group, and while volunteering with the children's/youth ministries at Newport Mesa Church on Sunday mornings. But even then, I spent hundreds of cumulative hours just standing there in the same room away from everybody. To reiterate, I usually feel invisible. Asperger's deceives me into thinking that others are ignoring me. Sometimes, I never get to do or say anything but maybe a "Hi" once or twice max. Everybody seems too preoccupied with their conversations and their videogames. I do not want to be interrupting them. People angrily told me to go away when I was really young. I have also been teased and given a hard time a lot. People ridiculed me just for talking. Am I merely holding on to those memories? Probably! But that's Asperger's fault! I worry about having said something wrong. What if they get offended? What if they say, "Stop wasting my time" or something like that? What if…?

When I *did* get to talk with friends, I nonetheless enjoyed their company while it lasted. Sometimes, it was only a "Hi. How are you?"

Now, it is time to turn the tables.

I *enjoy* spending time with others. I am not saying that I am entirely introverted and shy. It is simply easier in a more amicable ambiance, when lots of my friends are there. I feel more at home at social gatherings when more people know me. I prefer to be in a small place with more friends than in a large place with few friends. Nonetheless, I have acquired the courage to be densely surrounded by people at events.

Finally, although I never attended a Newport Harbor High School dance, I went to my first high school football game in my junior year in September 2011. Then another. And another. And they were actually fun, even though I hardly play or watch football. However, when people start acting wildly and jumping up and down, that is something that repels a person like me with Asperger's away. The soundwaves reverberate in my ears until I am dizzy. I may want myself to cower against the corner of a wall. Nonetheless, it was just fun to watch, be there among the cheers, and root for my alma mater.

In senior year, we all took a personality test that was required for the Senior Exit Project. Part of what I discovered is that I am an extrovert. Bewildered, I pondered about it. Then, I accepted it.

Indeed, I have preferred to be by myself before, yet I *still* have the zeal to be around others. I guess I always wanted a friend or a few to regularly help out, to talk to, and to hang out with. I desire to tutor those who are struggling with subjects at school—especially mathematics and science—if I know the material.

Therefore, I *would* classify myself in between an introvert and an extrovert, for I share qualities of both and am an "ambivert," as it is called. I do not want to be completely devoid of social interactions.

I would, in fact, consider myself sociable, but more nervous than the average person. I feel that I have successfully been able to break away from this common symptom of autism. Alas, there are more severe cases with some of us. Therefore I beg that children at schools will recognize some of these signs. I also implore for autistic children to practice getting out there if they are shy. I can personally testify to the hardness of it, but I have overcome most of it. *So you probably can too.*

I *do* enjoy large crowds but only to an extent. Importantly, through Royal Rangers teaching me several attributes, including leadership, I feel that as a commander, I have definitely been able to be around people calmly. My perseverance of becoming a teacher has also helped solidify my boldness and confidence.

I continue to perform in big shows and take classes in crowded lecture halls. After the HALO Benefit shows (Healing Autism through Learning and Opportunities), lots and lots of people come up to me afterward to compliment me. Likewise, several students usually come up to me after I juggle for their class. Thus, I do not cower when I am around a large, dense group of people. On the contrary, I am elated. I am jubilant. The bigger, the better.

Perhaps after utilizing perseverance (like with juggling and playing an instrument), socializing will eventually be a piece of cake. That is, it will hopefully get easier. I have certainly had a good start. I cannot see how it could be hard, since I have become my own advocate by now.

> *I can do all things through Christ which strengtheneth me* (Philippians 4:13).

I just want to conclude by saying that I treasure all my friends and future friends, as well as all the benevolent things that they have done for me. I would never *ever* wish to trade a memory. It is just that I could have employed much more of my free time to hang out with them, but instead, I spent much time by myself, alone.

13

The Peaceful Joy of Volunteering

For years, I have been both a student at school and a volunteer around the community, but as of the end of 2017, I have never been employed. I have done a couple of paid jobs here and there for friends and the church but have never been officially employed. I have filled out applications, but my workload from school has been a deterrent. I remember being fifteen and asking around for applications. They all said to come back when I turned either sixteen or eighteen. Furthermore, I needed a work permit from school. By junior and senior year of high school, most of my friends had jobs, not to mention a driver's license (but I did not get a driver's license until September 2017).

Since I had the privilege of R.S.P., I had plenty of training in resumes, applications, interviews, helpful tips, and so forth. In all four years at Newport Harbor High, a person from the career center would periodically come in to teach us new skills. Once, she conducted a mock interview where she represented what *not* to do, while another R.S.P. teacher portrayed the ideal interviewee.

Nevertheless, Asperger's syndrome has abruptly and audaciously gotten in the way. With the workload that school requires, I could not have possibly been able to hold a job. Even as a student at Orange Coast College, I found there are substantial loads of reading, homework, and studying—on top of attending class.

Because of Asperger's, homework and projects take much longer for me than the average student. An hour-long homework assignment may take me *several* hours to do. My concentration was essentially limited. Plus, I am extremely meticulous, which often renders me slow.

I *love* volunteering. It testifies to my willingness and sincerity, proving that my smile is genuine. I have been a Royal Rangers commander since September 2013. At our outpost, all of us commanders *never* put any of the dues into our pockets. We are never paid. It is strictly all volunteer, and I love that. It categorically *shows* our hearts. If we are being paid, then people may probably never tell for sure whether or not we are tolerating being there. For me, as a commander, to show up every week when we have Royal Rangers corroborates my word when I say how much I love the program and care for the boys. With that said, I will never *ever* accept a paycheck from my outpost or church for being a commander.

To date, I have attended every single Wednesday night meeting as a commander. In November 2014, I had what was essentially a routine endoscopy, and I went to Royal Rangers that night. In January 2016, I had all four of my wisdom teeth extracted, and I was at Royal Rangers two days later on the 27th.

I will always support and promote this splendid, outstanding ministry for decades and desire to witness it grow. Without Royal Rangers and what it had done for my life, I am sure that I would not be pursuing what I am pursuing today. I do not know where I would be in life.

For me, small outposts can be quite lonely, but in September 2016, our census started to skyrocket again like back when I was in the program. My hope is that *all* outposts worldwide, including ours, will be completely maxed out. Royal Rangers has taught me vital life skills, and now, I want to give back and impart them to the boys who are at the age that I once was. That is my joy. And being a *volunteer* attests to that.

In February 2010, one of the Assistant Usher Chairs at St. Andrew's Presbyterian Church came down to the high school youth group. He told us about the ushering program and was wanting to recruit some of us. In March 2010, I officially became a volunteer usher for the third Sunday, but after a few months, I became a weekly usher. In January 2011, I was promoted to Assistant Usher Captain and again to Usher Captain in June 2012.

Being an usher has richly blessed me. I made at *least* a hundred new friends in the church. It provided me with additional experience of sociably working with people, as I began branching out and away from my intrinsic shyness. Along with Royal Rangers, ushering has greatly helped me in leadership, as well as improving other inherent struggles from the notorious Asperger's. To list a couple of responsibilities, I place ushers throughout the sanctuary and am alert to be a first responder if/when needed.

Previously, I had volunteered to do the cameras at California Victory Church. I was trained in April 2009. Then, in June 2009, I was rehearsing with the children's church for an upcoming performance; I was the volunteer guitarist. Suddenly, a person came in asking if I was willing to run camera three afterward. I became flabbergasted and enthusiastically said, "Sure!"

In August 2009, after months of alternating between cameras one, two, and three, I began directing upstairs (i.e., directing the cameramen, operating camera four, and switching who was live through the computer). Working with the multimedia has been a wonderful experience, and once again, I was a part of an amicable camaraderie.

Years later, in October 2012, I was reunited with an old friend—the camera! I started going to Victory Fellowship, which is a relatively small, once-a-month church service in the afternoon. The pastor was a newly met friend of mine. I immediately began volunteering with the filming.

Later, from September 2013 until February 2017, I became the tech guy in the sound booth. Over these years, I would be doing a two- or three-man job by myself. That was fun. Often, I worked on adrenaline. Since I have Asperger's, my mind is focused! I sometimes cannot concentrate if I have to volunteer alongside another person, but other times, I could. Typically, I have a detailed procedure to do: I turn on the computers and projectors, set up the slides, put up the lyrics, and monitor the audio mixer. Needless to say, it was sometimes difficult to hold a conversation while doing that. Notwithstanding, I loved it. I enjoyed volunteering with the multimedia.

Once I started attending Newport Mesa Church in late 2015, I instantly signed up to volunteer in their First Response Team (medical/first aid). Continuing to practice with the technology of multimedia, I became a volunteer at Newport Mesa Church in both the AV/Tech room and camera one. It is nearly exactly what I was doing at California Victory Church back when I was thirteen and fourteen: cameras and directing. Hopefully, I will get to use their audio mixer too one day.

The two main categories of songs that I enjoy playing over anything else are hymns and Christmas carols. In fact, like several people, Christmas is my all-time favorite time of the year. I love Christmastime. I love listening to the holiday music, as well as ushering at the concerts and a couple of the Christmas Eve services at St. Andrew's Presbyterian.

However, it could be infested with pressure. Every single December, my heart yearns to have a fully-filled monthly calendar. I want to spend the most time as I possibly can with other people. Christmastime is roughly one-twelfth of an entire year. Therefore, I always endeavor to make the most of it. I persevere to volunteer whenever and wherever I can, and as often as I can. That is my earnest prayer to God every year. I loathe when I spend quite a few days in December entirely inside the house. It notifies me that I simply have not yet fulfilled my entire dream. My stress is the desire to have most days occupied with something. My topmost ambition is to make sure that I will have many places to both fellowship and play Christmas carols on the piano at.

Here is a noteworthy point—whether it is Christmastime or *any* of the twelve months of a year, I am a person who *has* to have involvement. I *need* to continue to volunteer (or work someday). I am sincerely thankful to God for what He has led me to do so far.

I characteristically cannot enjoy being seated at a pageant or talent show that I am not a part of. My mind diverts my focus on the desire to be *a part* of something. I have to be standing in the back to help out, even if it is monitoring. I have to be ushering. I have to be moving. Volunteering (or working) is seemingly how I function best. I need the excitement that I will be called up at any time to speak or play piano for a few minutes. I have to be ready to work somewhere in the multimedia at the last minute or render first aid or CPR. I feel that I need to be the guy who gets to assist in trauma or medical emergencies (depending on my level of training, of course).

Essentially, I *need* to help out in some way I can, whether it is in front of hundreds in an auditorium or behind the scenes. Otherwise, I cannot sit still at a concert or church service or classroom or anywhere.

I volunteered at several more places than those I have listed, and I would not trade it for anything. However, I was still adamant at wanting a *job*—something to finally earn wages. There have been rare instances when I was paid for the services that I had done with the multimedia. Additionally, for two months, I was paid to be the sound editor at California Victory Church.

The first application that I submitted was for a job as a health assistant for Newport Mesa Unified School District (NMUSD) back in 2014. Since I am an Emergency Medical Responder and am passionate to help people, I ventured off solo and just gave it a shot. Even though I was ultimately turned down for not having the minimal amount of experience, this aided in proving to myself that I can sociably branch out and inquire about a job, especially on my own.

By late 2015, it was time to try again. I went to the St. Andrew's Presbyterian Church's website and looked under the current openings for jobs. One sounded perfect for me: Assistant Teacher during the week. Since I also have tenacious passions to teach, I researched what would be expected of me. Previously, I spent *years* trying to volunteer on Sunday morning for the children's ministry, but it did not work out; my main focus was to *teach* children there.

(At least I had an easier time at Newport Mesa Church with getting involved in Sunday school. In 2016, I started volunteering at JBQ (Junior Bible Quiz) and the Sunday school for the fifth to eighth graders. While I had the joy of teaching at JBQ plenty of times, I have not yet been asked to teach or give a devotion to the fifth to eighth graders, much less play the keys since they do not typically have one weekly.)

Promptly, I filled out the application for St. Andrew's Presbyterian and called a few commanders for references. In early 2016, my family prayed together that I would get this job—it would be my first, official one. Weeks went by and I ultimately found out that they never received my application, so I filled the entire application out again and resent it. I went over to their offices a couple of times and sent emails. Nowadays, my Asperger's has bestowed leeway on me, giving me the freedom to now successfully become more assertive in cases like these.

Finally, I got an email back. It said that the job had already been filled. Disappointed? Of course. But nevertheless, it was an outstanding experience for me. I now have the confidence to handle any application and interview, despite having Asperger's.

In the spring of 2018, I felt that I should try again. This time, I looked into a job position for the OC Fair & Events Center. I figured that it would be the perfect summer job. My grandfather, mother, and I went to the Orange County Fair all the time in the late 1990s but stopped going regularly around 2005. The last time that I had been there was on my sixteenth birthday.

In May 2018, I officially submitted an application for Carnival Ticket Seller. Out of all the different positions that I had looked into, I thought that would be the most perfect one for me.

I subsequently got interviewed over the phone, and I was officially interviewed in person on June 10, 2018—a date I will never forget. It was my first ever job interview. I walked into the administration building on that Sunday afternoon and waited to be called in. Soon, another interviewee and I went in and took a simple math test about the costs of tickets and rides, and making change. When I handed in the test, I laughed, "I was waiting for the Calculus questions," since I got a B in Calculus 2 a month prior.

Following the test was the question portion. We were before a panel of four interviewers. They were extremely flexible and nice to me, knowing that this would be my first job. I had experience before selling things for Royal Rangers but had neither dealt with "rude customers" before nor had any major confrontations. I did, however, speak on what I would do in such hypotheticals and explained the importance of punctuality.

The other interviewee (who had years of working experience herself) and I waited outside as the interviewers deliberated. We were called back in a short time later and both offered the job if we wanted to accept it!

My fellow interviewee turned toward me and congratulated me since I had just gotten my first job!

After training and orientation early that July, it was time to start working. July 13, 2018 would go down as one of the most important dates in my life. From then till August 12th, I worked most days of the OC Fair as a ticket seller.

After a few customers, I rapidly got the hang of things. I gained more knowledge and experience through this job. Very soon after, I was prepared to handle anybody that came to my booth and found answers to give to any question that came my way. In a couple instances, I was in the two-person booth solo for a short time. I mostly worked the closing shift and was there till around midnight. We usually worked in multiple booths throughout our shifts.

Whether in the booth or out, I ran into quite a few friends of mine by surprise. I also made many new friends there with several of my fellow employees, my leads, my supervisors, and the security officers. It became a cordial, affable camaraderie.

I loved what I did—selling tickets and answering questions—but I also loved juggling for passersby during my breaks and showing coin tricks to the children. Some of their reactions were priceless.

Once my leads and supervisors found out that I could juggle, they requested that I juggle for them and all the other ticket sellers on my shift. After our daily briefing and before being deployed to our booths, I was called up and gave a short juggling performance. They loved it and gave me a thank you card signed by a lot of them.

The summer of 2018 became the most fun and memorable summer in my life! I came to that realization quickly. It was the best job that I could have had at the time. It was a short commute and flexible with my school schedule. I was concurrently taking a weight lifting class at Orange Coast College three days a week, plus an online Health class.

A scholarship opportunity was offered for the employees called the "Employee Spirit Award." The theme was "I Did It!" Along with almost seventy others, I submitted an essay about my greatest accomplishment and how I overcame obstacles to do so. For mine, I had written a three-page essay about my accomplishment in not only earning the Gold Medal of Achievement—despite the obstacle of Asperger's syndrome—but that I had been able to come back as a commander and give back with all my heart to boys.

The ceremony was held on August 11, 2018 in the same room where I was interviewed. Out of everybody who submitted an essay, I was one of twenty who received the scholarship. At the instant my name was called and people started clapping, I gave thanks to God.

Having this job was one of the biggest blessings of my life, and I will never forget any part of it.

Volunteering is my zeal. People who volunteer show their heart to everybody and attest to their love for it. I am therefore proud to say that I am a volunteer. Yet, whether it be another job or my career, I aspire to be employed again one day. I refuse to give up on that dream.

14

JUGGLING AND PIANO PERFORMANCES

Special Education Tea

"Matthew, it's for you," my ninth grade earth science teacher at Newport Harbor High School handed me the telephone. It was a couple of minutes before the bell rang.

For me? I pondered. *Who would be calling for me?*

"Hello?" I questioned in a quandary.

"Hi, Matt," said a familiar voice.

"Oh, hello," I replied to my R.S.P. teacher.

She asked me to come and juggle for the Special Education Tea that was coming up. I said that I would like to do that.

In May 2010, I got to go before principals and special education teachers from NMUSD, and juggle for them. NMUSD stands for Newport Mesa Unified School District. I got up to five jugglebugs (the cubed beanbags that I juggle) and three clubs...but *not* at the same time. I recited all current forty-four presidents while juggling the clubs too.

Since I entered high school, I started juggling in front of people a lot more. With my Asperger's syndrome personally, I am both extroverted *and* introverted; I love talking and getting up in front of people, but I am shy when it comes to socializing with my peers.

Subsequently, I was invited the following year to juggle again. On this occasion, I ran into my former principal from Newport Heights Elementary School. He was the person who encouraged me in sixth grade by saying, "You should juggle four." Enthusiastically, he invited me over to juggle in a small assembly at Newport Heights Elementary. Accordingly, in June 2011, I got to juggle for the entire second grade in the multipurpose room. Suddenly, I was asked if I wanted to juggle for the entire sixth grade too.

"Yes," I said in a heartbeat, without giving it a second thought.

I got requested back for the Special Education Tea for my final two years of high school. I changed it a bit in May 2012 when I played the piano, but I was back to juggling in June 2013. Furthermore, I got to be co-MC during senior year and got my picture in the OC Register.

Juggling in Schools

"Why don't you come in and juggle for my students? Stop by anytime," my former third-grade teacher said in the fall of 2010.

I always enjoyed visiting my former teachers, principals, and office staff. Even in middle school and high school, I would periodically visit Newport Heights Elementary. As time went on, like all of us, I had to say goodbye to several of them. They usually either retired, moved, or got promoted.

By the 2010-2011 academic year, when I was a sophomore at Newport Harbor High, my former third-grade teacher was teaching second grade. He said that I could come by at any time to juggle for his class. Thus, in October 2010, I walked over (we lived a few blocks away), and juggled. I could not foresee the magnitude of what awaited ahead, but that day was just the beginning. Subsequently, I came in to juggle several times throughout that year and for years since. The teacher later started teaching first grade in 2017.

Every year, right when I enter the classroom for the second or third time, all the students excitingly say my name. Their enthusiasm each time has been overwhelmingly joyful. After dealing a lifetime with the trials of Asperger's, this has become a comfortable feeling of acceptance, which is something that every person with autism needs to find. It does not have to be juggling, but whatever their passion is.

Not only do I juggle for them, but I also perform coin tricks, rope/knot tricks, and card tricks. I am adamant about not calling myself a magician, so I invented the term "tricksician." I also went there a couple of times just to teach the students rope craft (i.e., rope terminology and knots). In May 2012, the teacher gave me approximately one hour to teach about Abraham Lincoln.

Again, with Asperger's, these visits further help me defeat being socially shy. I used to walk in hesitantly, but now I boldly enter. Step by step, I have been forcefully breaking away from bashfulness. Furthermore, whether I am at the park, at the store, walking around the neighborhood, or wherever, many of these former students remember me, wave, and shout, "Hi, Matthew!"

Remember how I always try and visit my former teachers to see how they are doing? My fourth-grade teacher moved to Rea Elementary School right after I was her student. Years later, I started wondering if she still worked at Rea. When I found out that she did, I went over there. It was the first time that I recall having been at the school since 2004. I only attended Rea Elementary for summer school right before the advent of fourth grade.

After I got inside and was walking toward the classrooms, I saw a familiar person walk toward the offices. I figured that was her, but she was too far away. She went inside the office door. As I stood there outside waiting for a couple of moments, she slowly opened the door with a shocked countenance. It was March 2017 and it was the first time that we had seen each other since June 2005. I got to come in a while later to get caught up on everything from nearly twelve years prior. I told her about what I was doing at church and college, as well as how all the teachers, former teachers, and staff were doing at Newport Heights.

In June, I was greatly privileged to be invited into her fourth-grade classroom. I had my jugglebugs, clubs, basketball, and soccer balls to juggle with, as well as a deck of cards, a harmonica and its holder, coins, rope, my knowledge of the presidents, and a smile. The first thing that I did was pull a quarter out of a student's ear. That was when the entire class started roaring. Later on, I showed them a math shortcut and then taught them how to do it; a couple of students came up, and they began to comprehend it. That was wonderful. I delivered my main message of perseverance to them, so hopefully, *they* will not give up on *their* passions.

Whether I am talking to an individual or an auditorium of people, I am always proud to say what I *cannot* do. When people ask me, "What *can't* you do?" or when I fear that I am talking too much about myself, I say that I can neither skateboard nor surf. I always felt off-balanced on a skateboard, and I presume that it will be the same thing on a surfboard, with the dynamics of water added on. I announce this inability with enthusiasm because I never want anybody to assume that I can do anything and that I know everything.

It is not that I am unable to skateboard or surf. Yes, I would say that I "gave up" on skateboarding, but that is not what I mean in my message. I encourage others not to give up on their *passions*. Skateboarding, personally, has never really been much of a passion as it has been to almost everybody else. I still cannot fathom how skateboarding is possible, but it somehow is. I learned how to ride a bike and experienced the tranquil simulation of soaring with the wind hitting me, and that is just enough for me.

After I was done with everything that day, I sat at the back of the classroom. It was almost time for the bell to ring. As soon as the fourth-grade class was dismissed, the next thing I knew is that every student sprinted over to me at a hundred miles per hour with pen and paper in hand. They surrounded me from all sides. I must have given twenty or thirty autographs that day as if I was a celebrity!

The HALO Benefit

I dedicate this section of the chapter to the HALO Benefit.

In the spring of 2012, my R.S.P. teacher informed me that one of the dance teachers was looking for talented students, and she had suggested me. I soon got to meet the teacher, tell her what I could do, and show her my juggling. The show was for the first annual HALO Benefit.

HALO stands for Healing Autism through Learning and Opportunities. It is a nonprofit that fundraises money specifically for families who have autistic children. Founded by a mother with two autistic boys and inspired by an actual dream, it is a show that employs dance to support these families, as well as to have everybody acknowledge what autism is and its struggles. Schools and soloists come from all over to dance in the annual show. Several schools created clubs and host miniature shows.

The first day was Sunday, June 10, 2012. I was just promoted by surprise to Usher Captain at St. Andrew's Presbyterian Church. Afterward, my mother and I went across the street to Newport Harbor High. All the rehearsals were on the same day.

"Matthew Kenslow," the person opened the music room's door and called out. Everybody in that room started cheering because they saw me during the rehearsal. It was my turn. I was escorted backstage and was about to go on. That was where my mother stayed, rooting me on.

Nerves of excitement covered me from head to foot. It was time for me to walk to center stage. There before me was a giant curtain. A video was being played on the other side. Those nerves imbued me even more, but as always, I fought them and used them for *strength*.

Finally, the curtains opened. The lights came on, and I began.

I talked and juggled, I juggled while playing the harmonica simultaneously, I had somebody call out a number between one and forty-four and gave them a biography about the president based on the number, and I played the piano. After I concluded, I took a bow. The audience cheered as loud as thunder, which was the culmination of the night—the acknowledgment of accomplishment. Elated, I always relive such evocative memories incessantly.

I was invited to perform the next year and every annual since. In 2015, they blessed me with a significant scholarship.

For a person with Asperger's syndrome, getting up in front of people is surprisingly what I strive for. It is what I am enamored with. It helps define who I am. It bestows on me the privilege to encourage others and grants me the joy to entertain. It is like a catharsis, erasing all the hardships and trials that I endure. And why I do it is to make people happy.

15

My Story in the *OC Register*

In January 2015, I juggled for the fourth annual HALO Benefit. After I performed, I went inside the theater to sit down and enjoy the rest of the show when a person came over and said, "There's a photographer from the *OC Register* wanting to interview you." Little could we have possibly imagined the magnitude of what would unfold.

After my first interview, the photographer met my mother and me at a Starbucks in February for further questions. We made plans for him to film me playing the Steinway grand piano at St. Andrew's Presbyterian Church. I played "Come Thou Fount of Every Blessing," and also was interviewed in front of the camera as well.

Nearly one month later, he drove my mother and me over to the *OC Register* headquarters building in Santa Ana. There, he filmed me juggling while simultaneously reciting the presidents, listing the first thirty elements (due to time, I did not say all 118), and briefly talking about Asperger's syndrome.

The photographer had been quite interested in the research on autism and filmed an interview with a doctor at UCI who specializes in such research. Furthermore, the photographer also found a list of famous people such as Albert Einstein, Thomas Jefferson, and Sir Isaac Newton, who all may have possibly had some form of autism.

He had become quite interested in how I do in a public setting. Thus, in May, he photographed me ushering at St. Andrew's. Afterward, we had another photo shoot and interview.

We met one final time in September at the same Starbucks that we first went to. There, we read through the entire article to make sure that everything was accurate.

Finally, in December 2015, I received an email saying that it is ready! Since it was late at night, I waited to tell my mother. However, I awoke to my mother saying, "Matthew! You're in the *OC Register* this morning!" Apparently, a friend in Buena Park beat me to it.

The date was December 9, 2015, and my story was printed in the Life section. This became a humungous story about me and Asperger's syndrome. It went all over Facebook, Twitter, and innumerable websites. The article is titled, "Being on the Autism Spectrum Isn't Holding Back Costa Mesa Man." Instantly, I became an inspiration for families affected by the hardships of autism. It was the most perfect day too since it was also the day of my three finals for chemistry, trigonometry, and astronomy at Orange Coast College. After school, I could just relax from reading, homework, and studying. The next day, I gave my first autograph on an internet printout to Ginny Carr, a friend of mine in Fullerton. I have since given a few autographs directly on the newspaper article.

Later on that day, I showed the newspaper to my former third-grade teacher at Newport Heights Elementary. At that time, he was teaching second grade. He was impressed and asked me to come the next day to share it with everyone. I got to read the article to the class and show them the video. They all loved it. Afterward, I helped out with their art project, which was like the icing on the cake. Whenever I get to either entertain or help children, it is a blessing and a joy in my life.

We are especially grateful for the photographer. He put hours of research, travel, interviews, photographing, filming, and a list of other things into this. He has been extremely dedicated. In total, this article took roughly ten and a half months to write and put together.

I am also very thankful to God for giving me all my talents and for this opportunity to share who I am with Asperger's—including how I am overcoming its everyday struggles, as well as defying the definition of what I was born with: autism.

16

The Royal Rangers' Christmas Choir

In the autumn of 2014, I was in my second year as a Royal Rangers commander. That year, I handled the second graders of Ranger Kids. During the second grader's first quarter—an advancement rank called "Lynx"—it is recommended to learn the song "Amazing Grace."

I suggested to the other commander that we take them up to Fellowship Hall, where I could play the piano, and the entire Ranger Kids would sing. (Again, something that I always wanted.) In November 2014, we started on this project. We had a few Wednesdays available to go up there and practice. Hence, I officially started the Outpost #33 Ranger Choir.

In the second week, right before we went up to sing, one of the other commanders suggested that we start singing Christmas carols instead. After practicing for a few weeks on them, we all performed them in front of everybody during Newport Mesa Church's annual Christmas Tree Blessing night. It was early December 2014, and that was merely the beginning.

Throughout early 2015, I continued Ranger Choir. It was initially to be held two Wednesdays per month before Royal Rangers began. Rarely did someone finally show up. On a typical session, zero brave volunteers came. It was quite discouraging. After such a disheartening turnout, all of us commanders agreed that we would stop Ranger Choir and only do Christmas caroling with the Ranger Kids during the fall.

Meanwhile, I had decided to take Music 115 at Orange Coast College (Fundamentals of Music) in my Spring 2015 semester. This easy class was an excellent review for me, plus I learned new things. It is like knowing something intuitively but finally finding out how things work and its terminology. It reinforced my skills and helped me improve on my piano playing. For one, I started recognizing and using more advanced chords, such as diminished, augmented, and sevenths.

In the fall of 2015, we restarted the Ranger Kids Choir for Christmas. By now, I was officially a Discovery Rangers commander (third to fifth grade). At the beginning of the meeting, after the opening, I would rehearse with the Ranger Kids and then come down to teach the Astronomy merit.

This time, we had a definite plan. We were to sing at the annual Senior Luncheon Christmas party in December 2015. Well, the Ranger Kids would sing; I did not want to ruin a good event, so I just stuck to playing the piano. Everybody loved them. Furthermore, we performed at Vintage Newport Senior Living in Newport Beach a week later. We started going to this place earlier that year for community service projects.

Likewise, we continued in 2016, but let me tell you about this particular year. First of all, there were significant changes in the church. Consequently, the number of Ranger Kids and Discovery Rangers greatly increased, although we lost several of the Adventure and Expedition Rangers in the process. Anyway, this meant more kids, which meant more voices. Plus, we were invited back to the Senior Luncheon.

Now, I did not underestimate these kids, so I chose two of the three main songs to be "While By My Sheep" and "Jingle

Bell Rock." The third one was relatively easy: "We Wish You a Merry Christmas."

The only reason why I chose "While By My Sheep" goes all the way to the very, very beginning. It was the night in 2014 when that commander—the commander who was one of my *main* commanders since I was a boy—suggested that we should sing Christmas carols.

He asked me if I knew "While By My Sheep," but I did not recall it, so he started singing it. I opened my eyes wide. I had liked that song since I was real little but did not know the name of it until then. In 2016, I chose it for him, but humorously, he never got to hear us live that year.

This song and "Jingle Bell Rock" may seem formidable for some people who pick out songs for children, but for me, I believed that it was possible for these Ranger Kids to do it. I am just thankful that the other commanders sided with me on the songs.

Now comes the annual dilemma—I cannot sing the songs that I chose. I printed out the lyrics for everybody and handed them out to those who could read, but for the most part, I have to rely on my piano playing to introduce the melodies that may be new to some of them. Yes, there are certain, classical Christmas carols that some of the boys have never heard of before, or at least are not familiar with them. At least I get to introduce them to these all-time favorites. Fortunately, a couple of the other commanders sing way better than I can.

After weeks of rehearsing "While By My Sheep," when it was just the Ranger Kids singing (no commanders), I do not know how to describe it other than it sounded like a prestigious choir. No joke, but they were singing impeccably.

As I was there on the piano bench playing, I was listening to them behind me. I thought that I was not there, as if something inside of me was moving my fingers to play. I just hearkened to the peaceful tranquility of the Christmas carol and felt a symphony of melodious joyousness and peace. This is one of my goals in music that I strive for—to have a group of people (especially children) sing along with my piano accompaniment in this way. I was awestruck! Afterward, I gave them a standing ovation. With genuine commendation, I complimented them. I endeavored to articulate how incredible they had just sung. Likewise, they sang the other two harmoniously.

Second, the senior commander started bringing all the older boys up there with us—even by surprise a couple of times. It then dawned on me. For those couple of rehearsals, we had *the entire outpost* singing together all in one accord in Fellowship Hall. It was melodious. Therefore, this turned into the "Royal Rangers' Christmas Choir."

On December 3, 2016, we had a good showing of boys who came. Practically all of the Ranger Kids had each song memorized and sang wonderfully. Before our last song, "We Wish You a Merry Christmas," the director of the Senior Luncheon shouted, "Encore! Encore! Do you have another one?...You do? Alright! Let's hear it for them!"

Just like the year prior, we went to Vintage Newport Senior Living again. In fact, there were Ranger Kids, Discovery Rangers, and Adventure Rangers singing that day. Before that, the Ranger Kids and Discovery Rangers made over seventy-five handmade cards together for those seniors. After Royal Rangers that night, the Ranger Kids' commander called me inside and showed me one special one that a Ranger Kid did. On this yellow card with big, green letters, it proclaimed, "I will love singing." That was the culmination.

I need to append that if I were *never* placed with the Ranger Kids back in September 2013 to start out with as a new lieutenant commander, then the Ranger Choir would have *never* started! Exclamation point! That requirement for the Lynx badge is what started it all.

I will therefore persevere to maintain the *Royal Rangers' Christmas Choir* and make it an annual tradition for scores to come. Hopefully, multiple outposts will join.

I have Asperger's syndrome. I spent my entire childhood recognizing the unavoidable symptoms and my teenage years learning how to deal with them. There are limitations, and there are unique skillsets. If I cannot sing for the entertainment of people, then I can play piano for them. I love doing so, but now and again, it could get lonesome without people there singing with me. My passion is with children and the youth. Therefore, for me to be granted this privilege, I am blessed. Plain and simple, I am richly blessed.

17

An Olive Branch and a Soliloquy

It was a calm day with blue skies in June 2014. I was walking home and decided to stroll through Heller Park. This is the park that I grew up enjoying. I noticed from afar two teenagers sitting on a bench. They looked as if they were in their first two years of high school.

Now, my inner tension started. How am I supposed to look? How am I supposed to walk by casually? In my mind with Asperger's syndrome, I cannot help but be overly stressed out in the tiniest of scenarios. I, for one, do not want others to think that I am ignoring them or being unappreciative. When I received gifts in the past, I became a smidgen apprehensive. I have received presents before, and some givers assumed that I did not care for them. They seemed to have thought that I was faking a smile. I *was not*! I endeavor to prove that I really do appreciate their gift, but I feel that I might have to overact to do so.

Innately, I may not always have my countenance conform to what is ideally expected of me in certain circumstances, even though I try. Likewise, I could easily misinterpret facial expressions, laughter, and the intonation of people's voices. I may misconstrue an olive branch to be a bow and arrow pointing straight at me. They may mean peace, but I might think they are upset or angry.

On the telephone, it is harder. With my impediment, I fear that I might sound differently on the phone than what my face is actually showing. Likewise, I cannot see the faces of those with whom I talk.

Back to the day at Heller Park. I was walking from Knox Place to 16th Street. As I approached the two teenagers, I noticed in my peripheral vision that they were staring at me. I just discerned it. For me, stares are intimidating, *unless* I am doing a performance of course. However, without an apparent reason, I cannot stand them. It drives me up a wall, especially when the person starts to smirk or gives me an angrily disapproving expression.

Basically, I *knew* that these teenagers were going to ridicule me. As I passed by them, I avoided looking at them. Unequivocally, as soon as I got about two steps past them, I heard disparaging laughter. I did not even utter one letter, much less one word.

Smiling inside because I had known that was going to happen, I was determined not to let it bother me. It happened before. I am simply different. As I got farther down the curvature of the pathway, I quickly glanced back at them. Unsurprisingly, they were still staring me down.

As much as I (and lots of us with autism) endeavor to let it go, we *cannot* really. I still remember denigrating things that happened in kindergarten, and I cannot get them out of my mind.

That night in 2014, I had spent a few hours in a soliloquy. When we were reading William Shakespeare's *Hamlet* in twelfth grade English class, we were taught that a soliloquy is a monologue of a character, usually in a private place when the reader/audience gains additional insight on the character's mind and heart, as the character speaks.

That is what I call my private, cathartic discussions. I talk about everything that I am holding inside from early grade school to the present. I pretend that I am talking to someone—anyone—like a friend. I sometimes rehearse how I would have confronted the teasers themselves. I wished that I could have had the courage to start talking with them and express how they made me feel.

They did not know what I can do. These two teenagers, for instance, did not know that I was memorizing the 118 elements or that I could juggle or play piano. They did not know that I earned the Gold Medal of Achievement—an Eagle Scout equivalent. They did not know how much I give back and the several places where I volunteer. They did not know that I could give a complete biography of any president.

However, I cannot comfortably just blurt that out. I *hate* bragging. I totally *despise* talking about myself as some sort of genius or somebody. If I am wearing my awards vest for Royal Rangers out in public, I still find myself walking with my head down sometimes or looking away.

Needless to say, unlike most people, disdain significantly affects me worse. You can shout at me, "*Get over it!*" but I reply that Asperger's does not allow me to. It is relentless.

Therefore, it is easy for *you* to say, but you might not yet completely understand the tenaciousness of autism and what it can do to the mind. You may tell me that it would be easy for me because it is easy for you, but again you might not have autism yourself. That is why I am one of several voices adamantly getting my story out. This way, I can be one more encourager for families with autism and one more enlightenment that assists everybody else in deeply explaining what people with autism experience and how we view, interpret, and piece together the world encompassing us.

Answer these: calculate the square of 5,054 in your head. Then give me the birthdate of our 23rd president from memory. Next, draw the graphs of the six trigonometric functions without looking at the answers. Finally, list all the countries of Europe, Asia, and Africa.

Alright, many of you can do some of these easily, but let's look at the ones that you cannot do. Why can't you? I can. No sweat. How can they possibly not be easy for you?

Well, I just assumed that you knew all the answers because I studied these subjects myself until they felt intuitive. You may be a genius at other subjects or skills that I certainly cannot do. Thus, what is a piece of cake for you may be hard for me and vice versa. Therefore, it is just as easy for me to answer those questions as it is easy for you to forget the times when you were bullied. I am neither saying that everybody without autism can easily forget these times, nor am I saying that everybody *with* autism dwells on the hard times.

For me, I cannot really control my soliloquies. Usually, when something deprecatory happens, I spontaneously recall it that night. (For example, perhaps somebody obviously ignored me or stared at me, laughed at me with innuendos, or mocked me via name-calling and told me, "Oh, grow up!") My mind seems to blow things out of proportion, take over, and I just go! I start talking and talking and talking.

Characteristically, the thing that initially offended me evokes another not-so-good memory, which, in turn, elicits another not-so-good memory. I cannot seem to stop them from coming! (More often than not, from grade school through high school, I had been distracted in class. Rarely did I start getting labored breathing, but it *did* happen! I sometimes had to resort to the tripod position at that point.)

In a typical internal monologue, I get down to my innermost emotions. I often recall incidents from kindergarten when classmates audaciously yelled at me to go away on more than one occasion when I did not even do anything wrong. I might as well have been giving a presentation in class that I worked a month on while most of my classmates doodled or fell asleep. In fifth grade, out on the handball courts of Newport Heights Elementary, a fourth grader condescendingly inundated me all year by calling me a derogatory name over and over again. Back then, I persistently imagined and wished that I could defy physics and fly, pilot a helicopter, be the best at a sport, or something wild like that—anything to gain acceptance as a person from teasers.

When I entered high school, it was like a brand new environment. Even though I was almost six feet tall at the start and towered over most people, I still felt small, relative to all the big, strong juniors and seniors. My physical education class in ninth grade just happened to be filled with upperclassmen. Thus, there were a couple of occurrences of belittlement and degradation. Even in my college years, one person in a thousand, who does not know me, could make me feel devalued.

Then it hits me! I run into a friend. I receive a cordial compliment from a person whom I never met before. Somebody comes over and helps me out on something. Guilt accordingly floods me from head to foot. I feel ashamed for getting upset over a few tiny insults here and there, and that is not a joke!

This is what I came up with: one remark, joke, tease, stare, or anything can literally distract me from a couple hundred benevolent friends. It could take just one second too. I also realized that I forgot some of my prized achievements that I worked extra hard on to accomplish, as well as my talents.

During an inner soliloquy, I feel that there will be some sort of a cathartic release of all that I had to deal with, even though nobody is listening. I wish that I *was* talking with *somebody*, because saying everything just to myself cannot suffice.

However, I did not want anybody to feel betrayed. What if the reality of dwelling on teases and mockeries will cause a couple of my friends to feel remorseful of being friends with me? I never want that to happen. I cherish *all* my friends and am thankful for them. From kindergarten until twelfth grade, I was friends with almost everybody in every class that I ever had. And they had treated me like a friend.

Again, as soon as I run into a nice person—which is all the time—I personally feel remorseful for letting little things worry me. However, tell *Asperger's* that!

My soliloquies could last for a few hours. I may start hyperventilating. It causes me to stay up at night.

On occasion, a miniature soliloquy just might begin if I get mad at witnessing people treat *others* horribly. I empathize with those who are hurt and start to make up a scenario of what would happen if I were in that person's shoes. I usually get ready to counterattack (peacefully of course) with words. Perhaps we will end up befriending each other in the end. Hopefully. It happened before with me and others. Other times, a soliloquy starts when I am reading a story or watching a movie, even if it is fictional.

Throughout school, I have been patient with some of my teasing acquaintances. I just continued to smile and be a friend to them. I did not get upset and fight back. Of course, with Asperger's syndrome, I intrinsically used to have a *much* more taciturn character when it came to assertiveness or defending myself. I am the type of person who smiles a lot.

A myriad of my friends complimented me on these attributes. One of my friends came up to me one time, did not say a word at first, and gave me a hug. I had no idea what was going on. The friend then backed up and said, "Matthew, you're the nicest person I know."

While I try not to allow insults to get to me, they can still remain trapped in my mind for years. However, some harmful innuendos have actually empowered me to try even *harder* in my talents, learning, and aspirations. Nonetheless, I question why they pick on me. I *know* why: a*utism*.

Even today, friends give me a hard time but never to be mean. I try my best not to let it get to me, but it often does. I try to hide it from them and persevere to keep it a secret. I do not want them to feel bad, stressed out, or compelled to go out of their way for me. Besides, I figure that if other people are okay with being given a hard time, then why can't I?

It does not work that way. I tried hard for so many years to be like everybody else, but since I know what I have, I learned how to *manage* the inescapable limitations. Thus, I need to admit to myself that even though it is with good intentions that a couple of people give me a hard time, my *mind* cannot help but misunderstand the jokes. Truthfully, *in my heart of hearts, I know that they do not mean anything disparaging about it.* Asperger's deceives me into thinking that others are trying to prove that I am gullible or something crazy like that.

"Crying Wolf" stories drive me up a wall. Whenever people do not believe me or they laugh at me while I am trying to prove something, I may start to feel muffled. They may not let me get a word in edgewise as though I am shouting through a lead wall. It feels like I am choking because it strains my airway as if I am being suffocated by cigarette smoke.

When people ridicule me when I am telling the truth, it just exacerbates the situation. I loathe the phrases, "You've got some wild imagination," and "I don't believe you." Contrariwise, when

I am wrong, I want to know about it.

When I am totally confident in what I am saying (like a date, year, historical event, scientific concept, and so on), and no one believes me, I get in a defense mode. My heart pounds. I may become irritable. I am suddenly on the quest to show that I am right. It may not necessarily be facts. Instead, I sometimes try and *prove* that I am capable of doing certain things, like having responsibility, as well as tutoring and teaching. I even persevere to prove that to myself sometimes. However, for some reason, I am more comfortable at establishing facts versus showing my ability and talent.

Categorically, I could misapprehend people's countenances and vocal intonations. Then, I could go through a soliloquy for nothing because my mind revives the memory of it.

My mind asks, *Do some people look the way they do because they are busy? Because they are tired? Because they are mad or irritated? Is it my impediment? What is it?*

People come up to me at times and ask me questions, and I feel that they expect a concise answer in one second; but with Asperger's, I cannot always give them one. Plus, my impediment and stuttering can slow me down. I start hearing myself say, "Uh…um, yeah well, the…" After that, I could be fine, but sometimes, the person who asked me the question might just stare at me, probably wondering if I know English. I try my best.

This brings me back to people staring at me. Everybody, I am sure, stares at everybody else. It was probably in the spring of 2014 when I started getting really bothered by it. I get so curious as to why they are staring at me. I have seen countless people stare me down for no apparent reason and not at *anybody* else. Sometimes, they do so for several seconds. I can only guess that it is because I may look differently or walk differently. I am, after all, naturally a tall, slender person. That is just one hypothesis.

In March 2014, I was walking in the neighborhood, and a few children started running around outside. Across the street, there were a bunch of adults at a party. Through my blurred peripheral vision, one of them, who was sitting in the driveway, had completely turned around and started staring me down. From what I made out in the blurriness, she was *really* staring at me with an angry face—as if she were watching out for all the kids. I did not want to directly look at her because I was too intimidated. Did I really look like a kidnapper?

In October 2015, I walked by a family. Immediately, I heard the little boy chattering something to his dad. The dad replied something like, "Yeah, he's a weirdo!" I slowly turned around, and the dad was smiling at me. Then the whole family turned and walked away.

Can I be misinterpreting these people? In the past two scenarios, there is an overwhelmingly higher probability that I interpreted them correctly. But what if, by some atom-sized chance, that I *was* misinterpreting it? (And these are merely two scenarios. Plus, bear in mind my opening scenario.)

I have not exactly mastered the skill of deciphering the meaning of facial expressions, as most other people can do. Some of them lead me to *assume* that they are ignoring me, which could very well be the case, yet could very well not be the case also. I suppose as of now, I cannot escape it. I do not want to inadvertently hurt *anybody's* feelings. I would like to know if I accidentally am.

Moreover, I would like to understand why people stare at me. Is it because they recognize me? Or do I look strange? Do they want to ask me a question? I am always willing to help anybody out, especially when it comes to schoolwork, if I know how.

I have had a few dreams about children and teenagers making fun of me, ignoring me, or tricking me. I guess that is how much it gets to me. As soon as I wake up out of the dream, the depressing forlornness is worse.

However, one day, a couple of children saw me and started staring. By now, I was preparing my mind for the worst. Humorously, however, I discovered that they were merely impressed at how tall I was, and I started laughing to myself.

Lastly, when there is a humungous event that I perform in, and several people applaud me and give me a standing ovation, it reminds me that I am on the right track. I should not dwell on teasing or scoffing because of the nice, friendly people whom I constantly run across.

By a factor of a trillion, I have plenty more things to be thankful for than the miniscule amount of things to worry over. I have two careers in mind, and I plan to pursue both. *That* is what should be one of my main focuses to look forward to. Meanwhile, I am surrounded by a camaraderie of amiable friends and family at church, Royal Rangers, and school. It is rewarding and an incentive to know wonderful people like the commanders, boys, and parents at Royal Rangers, the professors and friends at college, and the couple of schools where I juggle.

Why should Asperger's tell me otherwise? Alas, it continues to speak as if it has such a prerogative. Nevertheless, in the interim, I have been successful at turning its volume down. I hope that it will finally be totally mute one of these years.

18

MATH AND SCIENCE

Science was *hard*! I always loved and excelled in mathematics though…most of the time.

When we started learning about electricity and magnetism in fourth grade, chemistry and meteorology in fifth grade, and paleontology and fossils in sixth grade, science had gotten quite tough, to say the least. I could not even comprehend what "mass" and "matter" was. What on earth did the teachers mean when they kept rattling off such jargon? I knew and understood very little of science.

On top of this, I had three years of annual science projects to do, starting in fourth grade. They were a *lot* of work. The great thing about sixth grade is that we could do an invention as a science project. It took lots of time and brainstorming, but I finally invented a pencil called the "Easy Eraser" where one can just tilt it to erase. It was a whole new design and would take getting used to, but I contended that it would save time in erasing in the long run. Every student went up to the back of the room and shared their project. Since I go a tad overboard, I posted a flipbook, where I had drawn a short animation on how to use it. (Everybody gasped at that point.)

Simply, mathematics just came easier to me. After perseverance, multiplication became easy as two times two…literally! I would constantly create these *ultra-long* PEMDAS problems for fun. I soared through Algebra 1 in middle and high school.

Solving for variables, substitution, elimination, graphing, and so forth, became as easy as three times five. I flew through the midterm and got an A plus! A 100%. It was quite rewarding inside. Success.

I did not take a science class at all in both my years at Ensign Intermediate School. However, I did not have any choice but to still take the science exam for the annual STAR Test. I told the teacher that I did not know anything about *anything* regarding science, but I had to take it anyway. In retrospect, while struggling through that test, my head must have been spinning as fast as the velocity of electrons orbiting around the nucleus.

My first, official science class came in freshman year: Earth Science. I was extremely excited to be taking a science class. I walked inside the classroom on the first day in the brand new Robins-Loats building and sat down. The class was quite interesting. I did not retain everything, but I learned a lot. A friend and I were two of a few in all of my teacher's classes who got an A and ended up being in the same Honors Biology class the following academic year.

At this point came the days where I felt like I had regressed back to Newport Heights Elementary—where everybody else seemed smarter than me when it came to science. Overall, I retained very little in that class. Plant and animal cells, mitosis, deoxyribonucleic acid, the different nucleotides, and Chargaff's rules were basically the main components of biology that I understood.

No joke, but toward the end of the school year, I felt really discouraged. Truthfully, my mother and I were *so* close to calling a conference. I thought I might have to move into a regular Biology class. But *no*! I suddenly felt like I could do it, and I became adamant about it. I determinedly persevered and consequently completed the semester. Now, I do not know how, but after very poor test results throughout the year, I passed with a B.

After that, I became overjoyed that I did not have to set foot in any more science classes in my life ever again. Exclamation point! But suddenly, something completely reversed that.

I do not know where I would be today if we *did* have internet at home. I grew up with AOL since I was about six or seven. Around fifth or sixth grade, we canceled the internet. Then, we got it back right before eighth grade, but sometime thereafter, the modem stopped working. We were once again deserted of internet access. Well, not quite. We started going to Crean Mariners Library in Newport Beach for internet service. I did tons of homework there.

Incalculable times, we stayed till closing. This lasted for years and years. Frontwards and backwards, we knew their closing times according to what day of the week it was.

There, toward the end of my second year of high school, my mother found a series of books for elementary school teachers, tutors, and parents, containing simple, yet vital information about math, science, English, and history. I would not only read these books, but I would study the information over and over again as if I were teaching it to students. My zeal to learn intensified as I began self-teaching myself.

My science knowledge multiplied logarithmically from like a one to a ten. It became a blessing that we did not have internet for a long while, for if we had, my mother would not have found those book and recommended them to me.

The next summer, for Royal Rangers, I enrolled in a Regional Occupational Program (ROP) class called Emergency Medical Responder (EMR). My science knowledge proliferated exponentially again from a ten to a one hundred. Thus, science got easier for me to understand. The second day of class, chapter four, we learned anatomy. By that night, I had the heart all memorized, and within a short period of time, I could draw and label the heart *by* heart.

Getting certified as an EMR prepared me for various emergencies, so I aspired to work somewhere in the medical field. Now, I have a conflict. I previously decided to become an elementary school teacher at the beginning of junior year. Being an elementary school teacher and working in the medical field are two diverse categories, but my passions are incredibly, tenaciously strong so that I cannot choose one over the other.

I met a friend that August, and she suggested to me to look into becoming a P.A. (Physician Assistant), for she said that she prefers them rather than the doctors. (My second EMR instructor at OCC in the summer of 2014 told the class that lots of doctors only have time to spend two minutes per patient. Then, they go into their offices to do all the paperwork and such. They seem to leave all the fun and social-interacting stuff to all the nurses and assistants). My main passions are to *engage* and *spend time* with people and their families. And in the medical field, it would include such activities as taking the vital signs and writing out prescriptions.

Nevertheless, I can still engage with children and their families while teaching. Plus, I can still help make science, math, and history easy to understand. Can I ever do both?

Meanwhile, back in the summer of 2012, I had gotten inspired to add anatomy to my class schedule for senior year. Yes, another science class—the first since sophomore year.

In August, just weeks before senior year started, I added the class. I now had seven classes for the first semester. Health was a required, one-semester course. It came incredibly easy for me since I was a first responder. I believe that I got the highest grade in that class too.

Alas, I did not last sixteen days with a seven-class schedule. Near the end of September, against my will, I had a conference with my mother and the R.S.P. teacher. I was being pushed into dropping anatomy. It had gotten so that I almost could not have a word in edgewise. I *really* wanted anatomy and had been doing so well in it; I only missed one question on my first exam, and my teacher was impressed. My mother and the R.S.P. teacher simply did not want me to get too overwhelmed, but I was adamant that I could handle it.

Finally, I took a deep breath. After figuring out that I was losing the fight, I had to make a hard decision. It was probably the only last resort in order to keep anatomy. I said something like, "You know, I think each student only needs *three* years of math, and I already took math in my first three years. Perhaps, I can drop Trigonometry/Precalculus?"

My R.S.P. teacher paused and checked her computer. "You're right, Matt," she said. "So do you want to that? Drop Trig/Precalc?"

I breathed and said, "Sure." (Who would have ever imagined when I was in fifth grade that I would choose science over mathematics?) At least I can take Trigonometry/Precalculus in college.

Throughout that entire day in September, my R.S.P. teacher could not stop praising me. "Matt," she said seriously, "you've made a great, wonderful decision today. You were like an adult."

In the long run, it turned out to be a blessing. I was awarded Student of the Semester for my anatomy class on January 23, 2013. I had a free third period as well. One day, when I would have been in math class, I was asked to be in the yearbook and a video regarding juggling and my president's knowledge. I also had plenty of extra time to do homework.

That academic year, I was nominated for the Distinguished

Student of the Year award from ROP. Meanwhile, I tried getting into ROP's EMT class, but I could not take it, despite my intense longing for it. There was a time conflict with Royal Rangers, and I was more dedicated to that over EMT. Plus, time was running out to earn the Gold Medal of Achievement, and I was very close to it. I was turning eighteen that July.

In the interim, I filled out the papers and wrote an essay for the Distinguished Student of the Year award. Sometime after turning it in, I went inside the career center of Newport Harbor High. There, the specialist asked me if I had received a phone call from them regarding the interview round. I had not yet, but after school that day, my mother, in the parking lot, told me that she received a phone call from ROP. I was asked to be interviewed! I notified her of the coincidence: the specialist had just asked me earlier that day about it.

It was after school, but I wanted to tell the specialist. I thought, *It is a one-in-a-million chance that she is still here.* I started walking over to see if she was. Just then, she happened to be walking around the corner and toward the parking lot. The timing could not have been more perfect. I told her, and she was overjoyed. She specifically told me that she had not mentioned *anything* about me having Asperger's. She asked me if *I* did, but I did not either. Thus, for me to make this step, she said, is extra special.

I was subsequently interviewed on Friday, May 10, 2013, and three weeks later, my mother, grandfather, a family friend, and I went to the Costa Mesa Community Center where the ceremony was held. Everybody nominated there were in the one percentile of the thousands of ROP students that year. We received certificates from dignitaries, including a representative in Congress, the Assembly of the California Legislature, California Senate, and the Lieutenant Governor of California.

To my surprise, I was one of the few nominated who received a hundred-dollar scholarship. Shortly after, I receive a surprise card from the principal. I went to his office, and he invited me to the Board of Education of Newport Mesa Unified School District (NMUSD) on Tuesday, June 11, along with two others from the school. These other two, by serendipity, happened to be friends of mine since elementary school. They were also nominated Distinguished Student of the Year.

In mathematics and science, I simply find *patterns* in things, so it became easy for me. I accredit Asperger's syndrome for this. But more importantly, I give the full praise to God. He has a unique calling for me in my life, just like He has a unique calling for everybody. On April 6, 2014, at California Victory Church, I went up to one of the pastors. He profoundly said that I have a calling into mathematics and that there is something with me and numbers.

God does not reveal everything at one time. I am currently in my early twenties as of writing this, and I still have not received the entire picture. For instance, I know that being an author is a part of His plan. It may be a lifetime before anybody really gets the full picture.

As I went off to Orange Coast College, I decided to go for an Associate of Science degree. At this junior college, my knowledge of science increased logarithmically again from a one hundred to a one thousand, and it will soon magnify to a million. Calculus 1 has been extremely intuitive to me, and therefore, I earned an A. Calculus 2 has not been equally easy, but I enjoyed it…mostly. I earned a B in that one; it was the only math class taken at OCC where I did not get an A. In March 2019, I officially received an Associate of Science Degree in Chemistry.

With my background of struggling with science, who would have thought?

19

Honesty

Honesty is a key life virtue. As a Royal Ranger, I pledge every meeting to live by the Ranger Code. The Ranger Code is comprised of eight blue points. The third one is to be honest.

Forthrightly, in general, I cannot stand the thought of cheating in a game, lying about something, being disobedient to someone, using profanity, plagiarizing, or stealing anything.

As for jeopardizing a disposition of integrity, I have been asked by people to do dishonest things for them. I could not help but become sympathetic toward a fellow student's rhetoric, but I have since learned to decipher when people were sincere or trying to back me into a corner.

Contrite about it and ashamed to admit it, yet acknowledging that I am human, I have been dishonest before on my own accord. Surprisingly, when we learned our multiplication table in third grade, I tried to keep the answers written down on a tiny piece of paper in my desk, but I did not get away with it for five seconds! My simple test was promptly confiscated because I resorted to cheating. I am actually quite thankful to have been in the midst of a lot of honest students. After the mission of drilling myself, I was able to memorize the entire 12x12 multiplication table.

Then we learned division—oh my goodness! It was very complicated to me at first. Suddenly, there was something called "long division." Once more, I practiced and became exceptionally good at it. The inner rewarding feelings of success and a better conscience were my top incentives. Getting the right answers made me further acknowledge that mathematics *can* be done without cheating.

Now it is off to reading! In fourth grade, I mainly focused on reading very short, nonfiction books, especially those pertaining to famous people and geography, for instance. During daily Accelerated Reading, we read a book from the library and took a test once we finished. If the classroom computers were full, we went to the computer lab.

One day in the computer lab, I had a miniature confrontation. I will never forget it. There was a question that I had forgotten the answer to. Having Asperger's, I extremely endeavor to be a perfectionist. Leaning down on the floor from my chair, I started to do something surreptitiously.

"...Matthew? Does your teacher allow you to look inside your book while you take your test?" a voice asked.

I'm caught, I thought as I turned around. "No," I replied.

"Well, I just saw you looking through your book."

It was the principal of Newport Heights Elementary. He had been talking right next to me to one or two other people who were working. I know. What must have I been thinking? I simply became still in the midst of a momentary, awkward silence.

Even if some people do get away with things physically, it will still linger in their conscience. With that said, since fourth grade, I felt that if I did something wrong, then my mind and conscience would never let me hear the end of it ever. This decision was actually influenced by a preview to an upcoming interview of some sort on television. After being told the details of what it was about, I made sure that I would not cheat (even accidentally). What if I got one extra point that I did not deserve?

Will I dwell about it when I am eighty and ninety years old?

During a test in drama class in freshman year, we had to recall vocabulary terms without a word bank. I got down to the last question that I needed to answer. It was so simple, but I could not think of the word. As I was scrambling my brain to catch it and reel it in, some person behind me had to say the word: "beat." It was only loud enough for a few of us to hear it.

Of course, I thought, as I instantly remembered. Now, there was a problem. It was irreversible that I overheard what that student said. Sure, it was not my fault, and certainly, it may have been okay considering, but just to be prudent, I believe I turned the test in with that question left blank. I just could not bear the thought of feeling ashamed about it for years.

In Honors Biology during sophomore year, we had four Natural History Reports to do. Additionally, each of us had to choose one between a solo bug collecting project, a solo plant collecting project, and a larger two-student project. I completely misconstrued the information. It sounded like the Natural History Report was synonymous with this larger project. Soon, it was time for the class to turn in their first Natural History Report. Confused, I went up to my teacher and found out the misunderstanding. However, later on, my teacher gave me full credit on it according to School Loop, but I never did it. I went up to him and explained.

"Oh," he looked surprised. "Thank you."

As I was turning to walk away, he appended, "You know what…for being honest, I'll just give you the full credit."

For me being honest, it is important to note that the reward was not so much the points. Rather, it was a clear conscience. It was better than my conscience yelling at me for the next century.

That famous saying, "Oh what a tangled web we weave,

when first we practice to deceive," applies to *anything* dishonest. And truthfully, that *is* the truth.

I cannot stand the thought of misguiding somebody or falsifying something for anything. Dishonesty is humiliating. I will neither say that I could do stuff that I cannot, nor pretend to know things that I was unaware of. I know that I would always be put to the test one day. So why do it to begin with? It will be detrimental to people who might trust me.

At Ensign Intermediate School, I was rewarded for not stealing. I had found unexpired lunch tickets a few times and turned them in to the cafeteria. They gave me a free, fifty-cent cookie.

In April 2008, with all the other students, I was rushing off to our first-period class. By the cafeteria, I looked down on the ground and saw a folded twenty dollar bill in plain sight. I was as shocked as if I saw gold. I slowly knelt down to pick it up. I opened it up and found that it was actually thirty-two dollars. Instantly, I knew that it was somebody's yearbook money.

I knew that I had to turn it in. Apparently, it *was* somebody's yearbook money. The assistant principal, whom I turned in the money to, told me that the eighth grader was very thankful and would write me a card. To this day, I neither found out who lost the money nor received a card, but truthfully, knowing that this student was appreciative had sufficed.

In summary, I accordingly dwell excessively on the hypotheticals. I not only recall my own punitive repercussions that I had to pay for several times in elementary school but other people's penalties as well. These "other people" that I am referring to could be personal acquaintances, real people on the news or talk shows, or characters in books, television shows, and movies.

Since it is hard for me to forget, I always considered a playlist of ramifications. By fifth grade, I was nearly unrecognizable to my younger self. That came through discipline and perseverance. I grasped that if I really try, I *can* accomplish things on my own.

I realized that it is a much calmer life when we are honest with ourselves in place of the burdensome, perpetual, remorseful conscience over our mind and body.

20

College Life

On Tuesday, August 27, 2013, I began my first semester at Orange Coast College. Because of having Asperger's syndrome, I received special accommodations via the special services, including priority registration, tutoring, and extra time on tests. Now, since I am an adult, I became *more* of my own advocate and implemented further responsibility. I purchase my own scantrons (which were needed to take most of my exams) and textbooks, search and sign up for my own classes, and go in to make counseling appointments and schedule test dates. High school had been a great practice; now, college is like the real world. It is sort of surreal and kind of fun simultaneously.

I learned advocacy straight from my R.S.P. class at Newport Harbor High School. For four years, I practiced it and improved. I practiced how to speak for myself and not require others to do it for me.

I will never forget the time when I took Emergency Medical Responder at Coastline ROP in the summer of 2012, right after junior year of high school. It was actually one of my first exposures to college life: breaks in the middle of class and no school bell; we could leave early if we finished. Anyway, I needed to inform my EMR instructor about the extra time that I might need for quizzes and tests. One day toward the beginning of the course, I told him outside the classroom door during the break. He smiled and understood.

May my R.S.P. teacher be proud of me! I thought to myself in jubilation. In fact, I only had to take advantage of the extra time once: the final in July.

By the time I started Orange Coast College, my issues with Asperger's had substantially lessened, but they were still lingering. Reading is still the most difficult of them all. Nevertheless, I met a friend there in the Spring 2014 semester who said that he cannot see me as a disabled student. My impediment was barely noticeable, and I spoke more clearly and concise.

I previously took the placement exam and was placed in Math 030 (Intermediate Algebra) and English 099. Taking Math 030 turned out to be another blessing. It was something that seemed redundant and unneeded at first, but it was a splendid review of not only Algebra 1 but also Algebra 2. I gained the needed refresher course of the conic section, logarithms, binomial expansion, and more. It had, after all, gotten tough toward the end of junior year back in high school.

As a result, I was all ready for Math 115 (College Algebra) the next semester. The class started in the early morning in January 2014. Being a nonconformist to the opinions of lots of people, I found that algebra has been very fun. I needed a twenty percent on the final to get a B and a sixty percent to get an A. I did not even need to take the final; I would still pass. However, I preferred an A rather than a C.

I actually miss Math 115, but after several years of algebra, it was time to move on finally. A good, fundamental understanding of both algebra and trigonometry (which I took in my Fall 2015 semester) will certainly make Calculus 1 much simpler and easier. Take it from me.

As I was taking Calculus 1, I thought, *What's going on here?* Okay, there were some tough concepts, but the first few chapters of limits and differentiation became very easy and intuitive. Soon, I felt as if I have been doing calculus for years. The procedures simply jumped out at me as I was solving homework and test problems.

Yes, I admitted to people and my friends on Facebook that I know calculus is going to get more challenging. However, with the academic perseverance that I had since eighth grade, I will endeavor to continue studying and to try the best I can.

As a brief background, when I was in seventh grade at Ensign Intermediate, I kept getting B's and C's. Some of my math and world history tests came back as D's. Then, after my first day in eighth grade, I drilled and told myself that I am going to *listen* to the teacher and *strive* to do the *best I can*! And to *endeavor* to understand all of what I can physically retain. I have been adamantly using such perseverance and got A's and B's all the way till high school graduation. I got fourteen A's and two B's in eighth grade alone and made it on the honor roll a few times within all those years. It is through that testimony that I encourage several children with, but in the end, just try your best.

Over the next couple of semesters at OCC, I have been receiving emails requesting that I look into their honor societies. In late 2014, I joined Alpha Gamma Sigma (AGS) and was officially inducted the following year. AGS is an honor society for students with a 3.0 and higher GPA; there is not a specific major needed. Likewise, Phi Theta Kappa (PTK) is for students with 3.5 and higher GPA. PTK is a huge, international honor society for two-year colleges. On April 25, 2015, I was formally inducted in. One other honor society that I joined was Mu Alpha Theta (MAT)—the mathematics' honor society.

Later in 2015, I completed most of the core curriculum. I could finally focus on the science classes that I like, but I did not know what my major was going to be. I wanted to get into both the medical and the education fields, all the while working with children. There is nothing more significant than to know that you became the inspiration to a child. One of my most rewarding moments of accomplishment as a Royal Rangers commander was finding out that I inspired one of the boys into choosing astronomy topics for a project in school just after I taught the Astronomy merit.

Over the next several semesters, I mainly focused on mathematics, biology, and general chemistry courses. There were some fun times learning and being in a camaraderie, yet there were also pretty busy and sometimes stressful times. However, I continued to use perseverance and have gotten excellent grades.

One thing that I am super glad for is that I took chemistry first before biology. That immensely helps in my opinion; it makes learning biology a little faster for me. (Personally, I enjoy chemistry much more versus biology, even though most people claim the opposite.)

During the summer of 2016, important decisions were being made regarding my major and university. One of my OCC counselors and I had been talking for the past couple of years, and he really helped me out. He is very well aware of my passions and understands my predicament in choosing a major. He knows about my intelligence. He keeps saying how lots of people can teach, but not everybody has a complex, scientific mind as I do. Previously, on May 19th that year, I talked with Vanguard University of Southern California.

By June 6, 2016, I *had* to narrow it down. I was about to choose my classes for my tenth semester at OCC (my fourth year). I really needed to choose—and choose *quickly*. I was getting extremely close to deciding on declaring a major and where to transfer to. My counselor said that everything was looking good; I basically have the core curriculum completed at this point.

One morning, I reviewed Vanguard University's majors and one stuck out to me. It is very difficult to explain, but after glancing at all of them, I looked back at this specific major, and it just leaped out at me. Upon research, I felt like I made the perfect choice.

My counselor took out a post-it note and numbered one through three.

"Top three universities. What are they?" he asked, pen in hand.

I made the decision. "Vanguard, number one. Two, UCI (University of California, Irvine). And three, CSUF (California State University, Fullerton)."

"Alright," he finished jotting them down. "Top three majors. What are they?"

I took a deep breath

"One…Biochemistry."

Surprise! This was the major that I figured might be perfect. I researched both online and third-story Watson Hall, where they have tons of resources on majors.

"Two, Biological Sciences; and three, Mathematics."

I have told a myriad of friends and family about biochemistry and received all positive feedback. Nevertheless, I still wanted a smidgen more research, so I talked with a professor/director at Vanguard University. Afterward, it was quite clear.

On Wednesday, July 6, 2016, I made it official!

However, OCC does not currently have an Associate of Science (A.S.) degree in Biochemistry. Instead, there is an A.S. in Biology or an A.S. in Chemistry. My other OCC counselor and I went to Vanguard University's website and found that

Biochemistry is under their Department of Chemistry. Thus, I chose to go for the Associate of Science degree in Chemistry and take it to Vanguard University. I posted my major announcement on Facebook and instantly received over 100 likes/reactions and a myriad of comments.

On April 17, 2018, I arrived at the place on campus where I receive math tutoring. A couple other students were there. We all saw a bunch of staff members (including my academic counselor) pouring inside this one tiny room, one by one. I knew pretty much all of them.

"Oh, somebody's in trouble," the student across from me said.

"It's probably just an important meeting," I guessed in a quandary.

All of a sudden, a couple of seconds later, my academic counselor comes to me with a big smile and says, "Hey, Matt? Can we see you for a minute?"

It was for me!

Oh, my!

I surmise that the reason I felt reassured was because of that smile my counselor had, but still, I had no idea what this was going to be about.

A few minutes later, we all exited this tiny room, one by one.

"And don't you ever do that again!" one of them said and pointed at me…jokingly.

I always loved surprises, and on this day, I had been given one of the hugest surprises of my life! I was chosen to be DSPS (Disabled Student Programs and Services) Student of the Year. This included a scholarship award and a prestigious plaque. I was invited to the college's 60th annual Honors Night to receive it.

On Wednesday, May 9, 2018, I was the first to be called up after the commencements in the Robert B. Moore Theater. Before I went up in front of everybody to receive the plaque and scholarship, a five-minute biography of me was read. At least a thousand people were there. I am extremely blessed and thankful that they would choose me for such an honor.

And then it happened! Less than a year later, I earned an Associate of Science degree in Chemistry. My grandfather said that I was the first in the family to get a degree. He was perhaps the proudest of us all. I was accepted into Vanguard University of Southern California around the same time with the agreement to begin in August 2019. I had already completed nearly half my coursework at Orange Coast College, which I am thankful for. On Friday, May 24, 2019, I officially graduated from Orange Coast College at their 71st Commencement.

As of now, I aspire to earn a Bachelor of Science degree in Biochemistry. From there, I plan to get credentials to become a teacher, and maybe thereafter, I can become a Physician Assistant. (It used to completely be the other way around, but it dramatically switched in 2018).

Since eleventh grade, I planned to become an elementary school teacher more than ever, but by August 2016, after intense pondering and deliberating, I decided that I will probably pursue teaching at a middle school such as Ensign Intermediate, or wherever the Lord leads me. I was encouraged by others to consider teaching high school and college, but that is not where my heart currently lies. My heart is toward teaching and mentoring younger students to help them achieve their goals and find success in their life. For high schoolers and beyond, I am most definitely willing to help out, but as a teaching profession, I prefer to teach at a middle school.

In an elementary school, I can teach mathematics, history, science, and more, but I have to limit myself on what to teach. As much as I would really want to, I cannot teach college-level chemistry, biology, astronomy, trigonometry, and calculus to ten-year-olds. On the flip side, if I teach middle school, I can teach more advanced topics but still not too advanced.

While considering to teach at a middle school, I initially feared that I would have no choice but to choose a specialty to teach. However, upon research, I can actually teach multiple subjects in different periods. I may not be able to teach the entire course of U.S. History and Geography, for instance, but I can probably find some way to incorporate history, geography, American Government, art, and music inside my lectures. I aspire to teach various sciences and algebra courses.

Just as a tangent, I probably will not have the pleasure to teach Algebra 2, trigonometry, and precalculus. As much as I wish, what are the chances of having thirteen-year-olds ready to take trigonometry? Well, one of the commanders of Royal Rangers for our district was doing trigonometry in the middle of elementary school, so you never know. Perhaps once in ten blue moons, there may be a small, class-sized amount of students ready to take it; in that scenario, I will be willing to offer to teach them. Realistically, I could at least help out and tutor older students who are taking advanced mathematics classes.

In the meantime, I am obviously in the exciting part of the adventure of finalizing my future. I am very confident in my current decisions and cannot wait to see where God will lead me in this. Until then, since it is probably going to take several years, I can still try and help out children by tutoring them with their schoolwork, if and when given the opportunity, if I know the concept very well.

21

CHANGES

Changes are hard! Through experience, I am entirely aware of how changes are a big part of life. I know that I will inevitably witness a plethora of more changes as I grow older. They are like habits—some are easier than others to relinquish. Not every change is hard, nonetheless. However, either huge or minuscule, when something is attached to a personal, nostalgic memory (or a thousand of them), it gets troublesome to let go and move on.

Some changes that I have a hard time dealing with are undeniably reasonable, while others could be categorically crazy (or at least when considering my emphasis on it). When someone unceremoniously replaces even a light fixture, it is a change to me, or when airlines amend their designs and color schemes, when stores rearrange everything, or when businesses alter the imagery of their logos or products. Some changes are harder to accept than others. It is like a teacher starting a new school year with a classroom full of new pupils.

More changes include modifications to outdated technologies that are turning obsolete. With my own stethoscope and sphygmomanometer, I can take manual blood pressure readings, but in the actual field today, everything seems to be digital; it is as if you do not need to know how to take blood pressure readings the old-fashioned way anymore.

I am thankful for the technological luxuries in this day and age, but I still enjoy using my electronic typewriter, telling time with my pocket watch, and referring to old books that were printed decades and scores before I was born. I cherished listening to vintage phonograph records back when we used to have a working record player. I enjoy taking derivatives, finding equations, determining concavity, graphing, and other things in calculus, but it seems that there are calculators for everything nowadays.

Currently, being only in my early twenties, I feel that I can literally start saying "Back in the day" about my recent childhood, for I was already saying it in my mid-teenage years. One time, I said it nonchalantly in front of a friend of mine who was in her late sixties. She started laughing because I was so young and she is the one who is supposed to be using that expression.

Believe it or not, when I see pictures of earlier technologies before computers, internet, smartphones, CD and DVD players, I get a feeling of nostalgia even though they were mostly used within years to decades before I was born. Almost any change—however huge or minuscule it could possibly be—is comparable to breaking a priceless, fragile heirloom passed down since colonial times or before. Imagine a restaurant not serving your most preferred, delectable meal anymore. Imagine your favorite dessert having a new flavor to it.

At Ensign Intermediate School, the mural that I painted in March 2009 was vandalized in 2015, along with six others. Therefore, it was promptly painted over and can never return.

One of the several most significant changes in my life that I still think about to this day was the demolition of the local Vons. It was more than Vons, but there was a Pizza Hut next to it and another restaurant known as the "Costa Mesa Omelette Parlor." Adjacent to these buildings was a Longs Drugs store, which has since been remodeled and changed to a CVS

Pharmacy. Each of these buildings used to have clay, concave, Spanish tile roofing.

In May 2010, my grandfather, mother, and I went to the Omelette Parlor for the first time in years. As we were leaving, we read that it was permanently closing soon. By that summer, the Omelette Parlor, Vons, and Pizza Hut were nothing but a pile of dirt and rubble.

I always wished that I dared to ask the nearby construction workers if I could have one piece of memorabilia (like one of the tiles from the roof), but having Asperger's syndrome, I was too nervous to make such a request.

Another extreme change (to me) was discovering that the building at Paularino Elementary School where my first- and second-grade classroom was located had been torn down. The slides, swing set, and entire jungle gym had also been rebuilt. When people tear down or renovate places that I grew up going to, it is literally shattering a part of my childhood. With several parts of my home county changing, I will not be able to share with my future family how it used to be.

As a contrast to all of this, certain changes are, in fact, exciting, such as redecoration, a different seating arrangement, or for me to be promoted to a new grade or school. It was like a new environment or being in a different place. Its unique atmosphere created a change in perspective.

Even though I will miss the old Vons and the irreplaceable Omelette Parlor, I was excited to witness the new, modern-looking Vons being built. The few churches that I currently attend had been previously renovated almost completely a few times, and it was rewarding when the process was completed.

There used to be a small planetarium at Orange Coast College. I had the privilege of going inside it a couple of times in early 2016 right before it was torn down and attended the groundbreaking of the new, gigantic planetarium in June 2016.

Moving a few blocks away toward the end of fourth grade became another giant change. It was very hard to say goodbye to the board and care home. My mother had a live-in job there. At least the house is still there, and I often walk by it, but it is currently no longer a board and care home.

I am naturally quite observant of the tiniest of details, which is why I notice little changes. I point out when someone got a haircut, a new hairstyle, or a shave. I see when something is moved to a different location. In summary, I learned that I need to accept changes. I choose not to allow them to run my life. They do not have such a prerogative. There is nothing I can do to have irreversible alterations undone. It is like shattering a piece of glass, taking the pieces, and gluing them together in an impeccable restoration without any cracks in it. It is impossible.

I still clearly remember walking down the aisles of the old Vons (even while I was in preschool), as well as being inside the Omelette Parlor a number of times. If the city somehow decides to rebuild these two adjacent buildings (down to the last detail), it still will not be the authentic original. It simply will not be the same whatsoever. The floor tiles, shelves, and everything else will merely be replacements. It is one-hundred percent analogous to buying a reproduction and not the priceless original.

Although I like a lot of modern architecture and contemporary music and such, I still want to conserve some of the picturesque places where I grew up at, as well as the things that I grew up with, the music that I listened to, the books that I read, and the shows that I watched. All that is left are the intangible, cherished memories, the pictures, and the home videos. In my mind, I can actually see vividly the places that are no longer there anymore.

As for me, I reiterate that changes can be hard and stressful due to the sentimentality (even today), yet can be exciting now and again. I understand that some examples that I described are reasonable, and several people can concur, but I also understand that others may seem too irrational. When it comes time for unceremonious changes, big or small, I simply need to take a deep breath and accept them, even though I will always remember what it used to be like…back in the day.

22

Conserving a Picturesque Heirloom

As I grew up, I enjoyed movies and documentaries that chronicled historical periods down to the last detail, such as what the famous person looked like and the exact words that were spoken. In my history classes, I enjoyed how we got to see old, black-and-white daguerreotypes, photographs, and footages of famous events and people. In twelfth grade, a guest speaker from FIDM came to speak in my American Government class. A few times, she asked if anybody could name a particular president by the picture that she put up on the screen. She widened her eyes in disbelief each time I answered. Apparently, I was the only student who recognized them.

The values of America, the history that America has gone through to get to how it is now (as of writing this), and its conservation are very important to me. I wished that all my classmates could have recognized those presidents. One of my classmates in eleventh grade U.S. History class did not even know where Missouri was on a map; I knew all the states at least by the age of five or six. As for historical figures, I want everybody to realize what America might have been like without them. We might still have segregation or slavery. We might still be English colonies. Who knows?

I grew up watching what America was like on television, in

movies, and in books. I went to the Ronald Reagan Library in September 2007 and to Richard Nixon's in February 2008.

I grew up patriotic, so to speak. Both my elementary schools from Kindergarten to sixth grade had us sing the great, classical, patriotic songs that define America, like "This is My Country," "My Country, 'Tis of Thee," and "You're a Grand Old Flag." I played "God Bless America" in my first talent show in fourth grade.

When I hear these melodious tunes and more, such as "Stars and Stripes Forever," "Hail to the Chief," and such, I instantly think of my home country. America! These songs epitomize us. They are just like hymns and the traditional Christmas carols; we simply cannot write music like them anymore. Our ancestors have been singing them and handing them down from generation to generation. Now, when I hear these songs, plus more classics, it hits me. I feel proud but also sad at the same time, and I may start gasping for air. I feel as if these songs are slowly becoming lost and forgotten. I feel as if my childhood was decades in the past, and I am now in a new culture, introduced to an entirely different repertoire of music.

I am extra passionate in saluting and pledging allegiance to the American flag. A couple of my few, all-time cherished holidays are Independence Day and Flag Day. Yes, Flag Day—every June 14th. It hasn't been celebrated much for several years, but I admire Flag Day. I like the idea of putting a date on the calendar where we honor the American flag. It evokes the traditional America that I grew up knowing: red-white-and-blue; country-style barbeques; small-town parades with marching bands; the wonderstruck beauty of the national parks; the picturesque panoramas of states like Nebraska, Wyoming, Kansas, Iowa, and Wisconsin; children laughing and playing in the parks; flea markets; a day without the stresses of work and school.

Unfortunately, I have not yet had the privilege to watch some of these events in person. All I know about them is what I have seen in movies, television, and books. I also have not been in a small town with wooden edifices, vintage cars, and an outdoor nursery of breathtaking flowers.

Flag deck was held every morning when I attended Paularino Elementary School. My sixth-grade teacher taught us the Pledge of Allegiance in sign language, and I still remember it to this day. In middle school and high school, the intercom would come on every morning. Everybody in every class would stand up, place their right hand over their heart, and say the Pledge of Allegiance. Well, almost everybody…

I was one of the first people to stand up; in some classes, several students lazily stood up. Some probably groaned. Then one day during freshman year in the art semester of Art History class, we had a substitute. When it came time for the Pledge of Allegiance, I stood up proud as always, but the substitute just sat there at the desk. I turned and looked at everybody. Some looked back at me and smiled (in a peculiar way). Others seemed to ignore both me and the pledge. I motioned for everybody to stand up. Only a mere couple did (and probably, it was just because I did). *Come on, guys!* I wanted to shout. *The pledge is just starting.*

I have never been so perturbed. It was quite an upsetting day (and this happened seven years ago, as of writing this). I have neither forgotten about this, nor will I ever. This dark memory of mine has bothered me ever since, and it keeps on popping in my mind now and again. I cannot help this due to Asperger's syndrome. That day, I witnessed an entire class—including friends of mine—who undoubtedly had no care or desire to pledge allegiance to their flag and their country!

Sadly, there is another distressing story that I cannot get rid of, even if I try. In late October 2011, after a big day with the older boys of Royal Rangers (when we hiked and set up snares), we got together at the commander's house, had a barbeque, and played video games. At some point, we sat down at the table and played a good, old-fashioned board game: Apples to Apples. (When I said "old-fashioned," I was referring to the fact that it was a board game and not an electronic one.)

I believe the adjective was "American." My noun was "Bill Clinton." I thought, *How can you get more American than an American president?*

When everybody had their chosen cards in the middle, my card was not chosen. Yes, *not* chosen. "What? How?" I questioned them. "Do you even know who Bill Clinton is?!"

"...Um, no," they all replied.

I nearly became as mute as Zechariah in the Bible. I was dumbfounded. Flabbergasted. Look, *all* of them were *born* in the Clinton administration. *I* was born in the Clinton administration.

I started giving them a miniature biography of Bill Clinton, like when he was born and when he served. It was then when they became impressed. Apparently, they must not have known about my knowledge of the presidents. I do not recall if I ended up winning that round or not.

For a long time now, I became enamored with thinking about living in "a panorama of the timeline" as I call it. It would be neat to live either a few days or a few years throughout the 1700s while both the Declaration of Independence and U.S. Constitution were being written.

It would be neat to witness a nation under the administrations of Washington, Jefferson, Madison, Lincoln, Grant, Theodore and Franklin Roosevelt, Eisenhower, Kennedy, Reagan for a few weeks at a time.

It would be neat to follow up on the stories from the Age of Manifest Destiny, the Civil War, the Reconstruction Era, the Industrial Revolution, and each decade of the 20th century in real time. It would be neat to travel from one momentous invention to another, to another, to another.

I would hopefully get to meet famous people and engage with the townspeople. I would get to wear the fashion of the day and speak in their vernacular. I would get to spend the coins and currency from back then. I would perhaps be able to be an apprentice for all the jobs and careers that I have a passion for (which is a plethora of them, for I have a zeal to learn). I thought about being a part of their communities and participating in town hall meetings, all the while helping out the best I could.

I just wonder this one thing: if a famous person from back in the day dies (for instance, an actor, politician, or veteran), then who in my generation, besides me, would know about it? That is one person less who grew up in the generation that I feel I grew up in.

23

When Was I Born?

Just to be clear, I was physically born July 22, 1995. That is categorically unquestionable. Nevertheless, I always told people that I feel as if I grew up in the 1950s in the country.

The logical explanation is solely based on how I was raised at home and at school. My somewhat odd sensation that I grew up as if I lived in the 1950s actually encompasses more than that decade. Nowadays, I can similarly append the 1970s, 1960s, 1920s, 1800s, 1980s and the Reagan Era, and even the early 1990s, within years before I was born.

I was raised in a board and care home for the elderly where, as I said earlier, my mother had a live-in job. In the late 1990s, the oldest resident was 102. I remember most of them. Inside this big, one-story house, there were usually five to six residents no younger than sixty-five. On average, I would estimate that they were born in the 1920s, give or take, back around the time when Harding and Coolidge were presidents. Most of them were my friends. Now all of them have died.

Within almost a decade of living there—from a couple of months old till a month before I turned ten—I had seen new residents come and go. Most of them needed canes, walkers, and wheelchairs. Throughout my childhood, I would practice using a cane, walker, or wheelchair and pretend that I was one of them. I felt that life would be simple, and I would have a quaint, daily routine. I endeavored to emulate how they went about their day. I found and used various supplies and taped them to my face as if I had facial hair. In fact, I could not wait until the day after my sixty-fifth birthday to move in as a resident.

All these residents were adults by the 1950s but not raised in the fifties. However, most of the great actors of television and movies from around that decade had been born roughly the same time they were. I was raised watching classic television shows like *I Love Lucy* and *The Andy Griffith Show*, and listening to music from around those decades.

I suppose I was raised in a very traditional way, and I am personally proud of it. We pray before every meal, and I was taught manners until I memorized them. Before I left the table, I was taught to ask, "May I please be excused?" I was promptly disciplined when I needed it. I remember wearing overalls. I remember hearing treasured hymns sung and listening to nursery rhymes.

My grandfather and mother took me to various places like friends' houses, as well as monthly gatherings and Christian events. Most everybody else was older than I was—from a decade to a few scores. All those who got to know me became friends of mine. Like my friends at the board and care home, many of them died too. And yes, I really miss a lot of them.

To summarize, I spent the majority of my childhood with those who were much older versus peers who were my age. I cannot be any more thankful. This allowed me to really get to know them and understand them. I remember going through books with one of the residents and playing card games with another. (I did have plenty of free time that I *could* have spent with peers, but with Asperger's, I was quite nervous (but that is a different story).)

I can be patient with them now. Some of them are slow in mobility or speech, while others are hard of hearing. Later on, I earned the Senior Citizens merit for Royal Rangers.

If you really want to feel how I grew up and what it was like, then watch the 1999 movie *The Straight Story*. It quintessentially portrays the quiet, calm, simplicity of life, similar to what I surveyed at the board and care home. All of that (plus gaining both respect and patience) are evoked through this well put together film.

Even though I never yet set foot in Iowa or Wisconsin, I feel as if I have been there in their rustic ambiance. A lot of my ancestors were raised on farms and in the country from the Missouri, Texas, and Oklahoma area. My grandfather is from Oklahoma but only lived in the country about ten to twenty percent of his life. He would always point out roadrunners, woodpeckers, and small windmills to me.

I watched plenty of television shows and movies that were based in rural communities. I visited several of them across Southern California in my early childhood. Some of my family members over here lived in relatively rural communities; some of them were raised on a farm. We traveled to several places such as Riverside, La Sierra, Corona, and the Living Desert. One of my earliest memories was in a rural setting in Murrieta, California, when I was one or two years old. Furthermore, I yearly went to the annual OC Fair, which has tons of traditional, rustic attractions such as farm animals, contests, and carnival games.

In this day and age, I further understand the famous times that the elderly have lived through. In sixth grade, we all had pen pals from people at St. Andrew's Presbyterian Church who lived through the Great Depression. Mine was born in 1928. At the end of the unit, we all walked a few blocks over to the church from our school and got to meet each other, fellowship, and have dessert.

That was not the first time that I had been to St. Andrew's Presbyterian. One Sunday morning in October, during first or second grade, one of the ladies of the board and care home would not wake up. My mother promptly called the paramedics and the board and care home administrator. After everything was all situated, the administrator asked me if I wanted to go to church with her, so I did. Almost every Sunday for the next few years, both of us would go to St. Andrew's Presbyterian Church. (That is probably why I later attended their youth group once I got into high school, which got me into ushering.)

If it were not for that unfortunate event at the board and care home, I probably would not have attended St. Andrew's Presbyterian to begin with. Then again, I might have later on.

The church is big and spacious with a balcony, a full choir, an orchestra, and a huge organ. We attended the first service. It was a traditional one where hymns were sung, and everybody wore suits and dresses. Most of the congregation were either middle-aged or elderly. I always enjoyed the few moments toward the beginning when we all greeted each other and shook hands. After opening worship, the children would be called down to the front for a very brief message before going to Sunday school for the rest of the service.

After a few years, I started attending California Victory Church. Likewise, everybody dressed formally, but they and the children's church usually sang contemporary worship songs. I enjoyed them too. I can quickly be taken back to when I was in fifth grade (and a couple of years thereafter) upon hearing artists like Chris Tomlin, Jeremy Camp, and Third Day, and songs like "Better Is One Day," "Beautiful One," and "He Reigns."

By 2009, there would be fellow members of the youth who came dressed debonairly in suits. My grandfather taught me how to tie a necktie on Valentine's Day that year. He had given me one of his suit coats in October of the previous year. So, in March 2009, after coming home from Royal Rangers, I suddenly decided to start wearing formal attire to church. The following Sunday, I went dressed up in a suit. I was excited and felt proud and distinguished; it always made me feel dignified. I even surprised my grandfather once we got there, plus many other people. When I first started, my grandfather and a couple of the men would periodically come over to fix my necktie. Ever since, I have dressed formally for church.

Once high school started later that year, I began attending the youth group at St. Andrew's Presbyterian. In February 2010, one of the head ushers asked all of us if we would be willing to usher once a month. I raised my hand and got the third Sunday. Therefore, I started on the third Sunday of the next month. Soon, I ushered every Sunday, which lead to my two promotions in 2011 and 2012, respectively.

It was not long before I realized what was missing. The orchestra! The choir! The balcony was closed! Everybody except for me was pretty much casual! What happened in the past five years? They did get a new pastor in 2009, but that was not it. I asked my mother about it, and she said that we were attending the contemporary service. *A contemporary service?*

We attended the 11:11 A.M. service, which was the third service of the day. The first one was the traditional service, and the second was the blended service. Both of these earlier services had the dapper attire, plus the full band and orchestra. Well, I decided to still dress formal anyway.

Over the next several years, I started to attend and usher at special, traditional services, such as Maundy Thursday, Thanksgiving, and Christmas Eve. I also got to usher at the blended service as well. *That* is where I felt at home with the hymns, elegance, and smiles. I got in a camaraderie with the traditional/blended service ushers as well, who were mostly older and all in suits. There were also a couple of younger ushers in suits for such services.

By 2013, I immediately knew that I was experiencing some sort of culture shock! It was genuinely a hard process for me to come out of the magnificence of the blended second service and go straight into the contemporary third service. Suddenly, I felt like a person living in the fifties being teleported to the new generation of the 21st century. The smaller band without a choir played loud, contemporary songs—just like at the high school youth group. They had loud beatings of the drums and strums from an electric guitar and rarely played hymns.

About ninety percent of the ushers were high schoolers (not that there is anything wrong with that). I made friends with them, and many went on to earn the Eagle Scout award in their troops.

People flooded into the sanctuary wearing beach shirts and short; some of them had flip flops on instead of shoes. Some wore jeans. Back in the 1970s, my mother saw a girl wearing shorts to a Wednesday night youth group. Shocked, she told my grandfather (her father), "Look at that! She's wearing shorts to church!" One rainy night, on February 19, 2011, my mother told a family friend about the contemporary third service of St. Andrew's Presbyterian dressing up that way. This friend would preach at a monthly Christian event that we attended. I overheard this friend of ours shouting angrily, "I wouldn't even let them in the church!" Essentially, my grandfather concurred with her.

For me, I felt as if I grew up back in the day. Another friend of ours who is also a pastor—and born in the same year as my grandfather—told me that *her* father always wore suits on

Sundays. And back in the day, *everybody* respected him while walking down the sidewalk, because back in that day, people respected those who wore a suit on Sunday for church.

Furthermore, people dressed up formally when doing relatively simple things, such as dining at a restaurant or seeing a picture at the theater. Plus, there is always something about movies from the 1950s, 40s, and 30s that adds to the picturesqueness.

As an usher, a few older people have complained to me about the loud, contemporary music. They stay outside until the sermon starts; then they immediately leave after the message. Personally, I understand a thousand percent. I grew up around hymns, but today *is* like a different culture. I want to preserve the nice, soft hymns like the first two services do. However, I like several of the new songs as well.

I can parallel this with both secular and Christmas songs too. I admire a whole repertoire of songs from the roaring twenties, the big bands of the swing era, the sixties, and more. Nonetheless, I like a lot of the recent and relatively recent songs too (i.e., 1980s to the present day). Likewise, the same thing for television shows and movies. Therefore, I am not a person who *only* enjoys things from the past but both past *and* present. Still, I am adamant in making history's heirlooms relevant. Like I said in my case toward the beginning, it was all how I was raised.

Since I play piano, I can play several hymns. When I would practice after church on certain Sundays at Newport Mesa Church, a few people came over and said nostalgically to me, "That's the music *I* grew up listening too."

One person cheered, "Yeah! Hymns!" Another person walked by and shouted, "You need to play for the church!"

That is one of my hundreds of missions in life: to conserve

these cherished songs before they're banned and forgotten. Thus, in 2017, I volunteered to be the piano player at a small church for the elderly, which is packed with the good, traditional hymns.

Like I said before, when I ushered both the blended and contemporary services back-to-back, I strangely felt empty and lonely. Plus, it is significantly smaller. I explained this phenomenon to a couple of people, including one of the commanders at Royal Rangers during a 2013 campout at Lake Hemet. In senior year, I started feeling the same way at Newport Harbor High and the high school youth group, because of course, that was contemporary. Everybody—even friends of mine—would socialize and talk about current times. Having some social shyness anyway, I was usually not interested in the conversation. At the high school, the conversations that I was overhearing got inappropriate too, which I have no interest in whatsoever.

I felt better when older, traditional people are present. (I am not talking about just the elderly but also the middle-aged). When they came to the high school youth group to speak, I felt more belonging. I felt that the person was a childhood friend, but I surmised that if I started revealing what I was hiding from most people to them, they would not understand. They would probably think that I was strange or something. Do not get me wrong, I have made hundreds of friends who were my age, and they have been nice to me, even though we hardly—if ever—hung out.

I enjoy many things: writing in both cursive and calligraphy, antiques, classic songs, movies, and television shows. I enjoy having very old books from the late 19th century and early 20th century and collecting old coins dating back to the fifties and earlier.

In eighth grade, I bought and started wearing a pocket

watch with pride. In ninth grade, I proudly began wearing vests in the style of a three-piece suit. Today, I have vests with pockets, so I enjoy wearing my pocket watch in my vest like the people in Abraham Lincoln's day.

In tenth grade, I watched the 1952 *I Love Lucy* episode entitled, "Lucy Hires an English Tutor." I watched it often. It inspired me to employ properly spoken English. I endeavored to amalgamate its rarely spoken vernacular inside the modern colloquialism of today. It helped me build diction and learn several vocabulary terms and phrases.

Once I got to say, "It is a pleasure to make your acquaintance" at the high school youth group. The person complimented me and told everybody there at the same time. Everybody started cheering and clapping for me at that point.

Toward the end of that year, in May 2011, at the annual St. Andrew's Presbyterian Church's rummage sale, I bought a Montgomery Ward electronic typewriter. It had a carrying case, a good ribbon, and everything. That night, I believe, I did my vocabulary homework for World History and Geography class while utilizing that typewriter. Although it was not the fifties, it was probably from the seventies.

In eleventh grade, after learning the vowels in Spanish 1, I brought in that same abovementioned *I Love Lucy* episode on DVD. The character, Ricky Ricardo, pronounced all five vowels in Spanish, instead of enunciating them in English as Mr. Livermore demonstrated. My teacher thought it was extremely pertinent and played it for everyone in all her Spanish 1 classes; she said that it fit perfectly in the lesson. I was tremendously excited to have a segment of 1952 being played in a high school classroom of 2011. Everybody enjoyed it.

Later on in the school year, a guest speaker from FIDM unsurely said something like, "You may not have heard of this before, but has anyone ever watched the TV show, *I Love Lucy*?" The entire class laughed like kookaburras, and I subsequently raised my hand.

In April 2012, I excitingly got one more accessory to transport me back to the fifties: a fedora. My grandfather almost did a backflip again. Back in the 1950s, it apparently seemed that almost every man wore this style of hat while walking down the street. My former Art History teacher, who lived back then, told me that it was the culture back in the day. I wore that hat everywhere. It was one more adjunct in conserving the culture.

I fear that when I start mentioning anything from the 1700s to the 1950s in everyday conversation (even the diction and phrases of the epoch), some might assume that I am joking or mocking about it in some way, as some people do. That may have happened to me a couple of times. On the other side of the table, if and when I become strict on traditional things, then I might be impudently laughed at and viewed as their father or their grandfather.

For instance, I am vehemently adamant that American flags should never touch the ground, that people should keep their word, that Bibles should never be treated carelessly, and that everybody should respect the teacher or whoever is talking. I favor military-style discipline, such as drill commands, formations, and marches. This is something that Royal Rangers enforces. I had started reviving it in our outpost back in the spring of 2015 with the youngest division. The youngest of all the boys got the drill commands down quite remarkably.

I would say that since November 2014, I strongly desired to support and defend my country—neither for money nor free education. Thus, in early 2018, I have gotten a lot of my questions answered when I went in and talked to a United States Navy recruiter. I aspire to do whatever I can to serve my country in the

U.S. Navy one day, perhaps as a corpsman or scientist.

Furthermore, I do not seem to always understand some of the prevailing, contemporary games and music. I was raised with traditional, rainy-day-like activities and games: arts and crafts; board games; card games; jigsaw puzzles; singing nursery rhymes; listening to classic stories; playing Duck, Duck, Goose, Musical Chairs, Heads Up, Seven Up, Telephone, Tic Tac Toe, Rock, Paper, Scissors; and other great oldies, even though I grew up in the late 1990s and early 2000s.

I have watched thousands and thousands of hours of shows that were mostly filmed in the 1970s, such as *Emergency!* I grew up watching *Columbo* and *The Brady Bunch*. Later on, I started watching *The Mod Squad*. It is important to note that I now feel as if I grew up in the 1970s simultaneously. Every time when I think about and watch these shows—especially *Emergency!*—it is as if I was there back then. I have this bewildering, nostalgic feeling as if I lived there back then. It was surreal when I got to visit the exterior of both the fire station and hospital from *Emergency!* in 2015. From a distance and even close up, they looked nearly identical to how they looked about forty years earlier.

It was even more incredible when I got to handshake, get autographs, and take pictures with Randolph Mantooth and Kevin Tighe in person, along with Mike Stoker and one of the directors, on July 14, 2018. It was at the grand opening for the Los Angeles County Fire Museum in the Mayne Events Center along Bellflower Boulevard. Inside the museum houses the original Squad 51 and Engine 51, among others. It was quite one of the most exciting, eventful experiences ever.

I particularly like *Emergency!* more, because it not only reflects the streets, disposition, technology, architecture, the wood paneling, fashion, music, politics, advertisements, and even the grocery stores of the 1970s, but it also magnifies my medical and desire-to-help-people passions. With that said, shows and movies that have doctors, astronomers, chemists, or other scientists in them as characters bring out my passion to study science. Likewise, shows and movies about teachers and schools evoke my desire to teach children. I like the thought of the rush of adrenaline that comes from emergency medicine, but I do not think that I will specialize in that branch.

As for the 1800s—and even 1700s to an extent—I enjoyed them because I was raised learning about the presidents. I learned some things about them at school, but I would *really* learn more about them on my own time, looking at their portraits and flipping through a presidential book that I had. I watched *Liberty Kids*, which was more about the Revolutionary War.

Here is my rational theory behind this entire phenomenon. Since I have Asperger's syndrome, changes are hard. It seems difficult to move into another generation. And the many generations that I *seemingly* grew up in were mostly the generations that came before me. This cannot be entirely possible without my memory (which also comes from Asperger's). From fragments to vivid detail, I can recall many things from at least the age of two and onward—what I watch, listen to, taste, and learn.

Therefore, I carry what I learned into the next year. Then I carry those two years into the next one. I thus have nearly twenty years of memories to reminisce on. Those things encompass the epoch of my parents, grandparents, and great grandparents. I always got to talk with older people, and some of them shared their memorabilia from their day. And since I cannot live exactly like them (in terms of history, among other things, such as the fashion and furnishings that are seen in fifties advertisements and shows from the seventies), I start to miss their culture.

Do not get me wrong. I am thankful for the conveniences that come with amazing up-to-date technology, albeit, I still like pocket watches, typewriters, and nearly everything else that were contemporaneous with them.

In summary, I *never* lived back then. I was not reborn in 1995 after *any* other life (or lives). It is categorically, unassailably, positively because of both Asperger's and how I was raised. Under Asperger's, it is easy to hang onto things, while difficult to forget details and accept changes.

24

PUBLIC SPEAKING

My first time at FCA (Fellowship of Christian Athletes) was the last "huddle" of the 2009-2010 academic year. It is a Christian club where you neither have to be a Christian nor an athlete to attend. (For me, I was not an athlete.) A good friend of mine had invited me. I started attending regularly during sophomore year and became a captain in junior year. As a captain, I met with the rest of the leadership on Mondays. The huddles were on Fridays. Both were held during lunch.

Then, the culmination of it all came on Friday, May 10, 2013. To set the scene, during a leadership meeting toward the end of junior year, a person suggested to everybody of doing a skit at one of the huddles. I was always enamored with both acting and public speaking. I suggested the "What Would Have Happened Room." This is a famous skit that I watched a couple of times when I was ten or so.

Although it was never pursued, I became determined to turn it into a skit where I could play both roles. Since I was entering senior year, I had the eligibility to be a student speaker for one of the huddles if I wanted. Essentially, my main message was about grace, God's love, and being saved from our sins, and it always came out to forty minutes long, give or take! I did not have forty minutes. Rather, twenty at the most.

At a typical huddle, between one and two hundred students would come and fill the upper seating of our school's main gymnasium. As a captain, I helped pass out plates and later, the pizza. When most people had arrived, a game started. Following was the opening prayer, the message from a guest speaker (usually a youth pastor, an athlete, or a veteran), and the closing prayer. I, of course, requested *not* to have a game, which could give me a few extra, valuable minutes.

I ultimately had to discard the entire skit idea and just give my main message. This significantly reduced the time needed. In the meantime, I had been memorizing more Scripture passages, which I remember to this day.

I continued rehearsing and timing my messages for *months*. I rehearsed nearly every day (and/or night) a few times back-to-back. I kept inviting friends and teachers. As for finalizing the quintessential date, it became an up-and-down roller coaster. I preferred an "A" day because I did not have a third period (long story short). Third period was right before lunch. That way, I would have just under two hours to rehearse for the last time before delivering the message for real.

The big day finally arrived after dedicating hundreds (if not thousands) of hours rehearsing. Five minutes before the lunch bell rang, I was on the other side of the school, waiting to help pick up the boxes of pizza and still rehearsing the speech in my mind. I brought a small timer and set it for twenty-nine minutes. When the bell rang, I would start it. Once it went off, I knew that I would have a minute to conveniently wrap things up. I was planning ahead for the possibility that I may not finish. My time frame was as unstable as the nuclei of radioactive elements; I had between fifteen and twenty minutes, at most.

It was getting to be a minute or two before the bell rang. I went over to an SUV to help. Once the bell rang, I started the timer. *Where are the captains?* I looked around, getting nervous.

Finally, a couple of them jogged over. I helped carry a stack all the way over to the gymnasium. On the way, I happened to see my R.S.P. teacher, the helper for that class, and a friend since seventh grade walking together out of the Home Arts building.

"Hey, Matt!" my R.S.P. teacher called out. "We're coming to hear you speak!"

As we approached closer to the gymnasium, a friend from eighth grade descended down the staircase of the Robins-Loats building and walked with us the rest of the way.

Remember that I requested not to have a game, but they did anyway. More people came during that time, though. After helping to deliver the pizza to everybody, I was all set. There had to have been over a hundred people there. Once I started, I kept going. It was just like rehearsing it. Now and again, it became numbing.

Whenever I deliver a speech, I can often recall a vivid moment of when and where I was while rehearsing that paragraph, but I do not let that distract me. Here and there, I do not physically feel that I am speaking. I am just standing there and hearing myself speak the words that are coming out of my mouth. It is as if I am on autopilot or something.

All my life, I loved getting up in front of the class and presenting. It is no wonder why I got the Public Speaking merit in Royal Rangers. Public Speaking at Orange Coast College was also a fun course since it was right up my alley.

Notwithstanding the exhilarating jubilation of speaking in front of many others, there used to be a notorious enemy who always came up with me. *Stuttering*. Due to my speech impediment, even my conversations are infested with the uninvited words, "Uh" and "Um," to name a couple.

In February 2011, I was telling a story in front of a lifelong friend of mine who would preach all the time. Toward the very beginning, she abruptly cut me off. "Matthew," she complained and essentially elucidated, "I cannot understand a word you're saying. When you speak in front of others, you need to talk slowly and loud. You need to pronounce your words." (By seventeen, I had significantly improved my speech and conversational skills.)

Bearing that story and countless others in mind, I gave my message that encompassed the Fall of Man, a brief timeline of the Old Testament, Jesus and His love and sacrifice, and recited about fourteen Scripture verses. All of this, I did completely from memory with no notes or anything.

About three-quarters into my speech, I tried to glance down at my timer quickly. I did not want to use my wristwatch or be too obvious that I was checking how much time I had left. I did not want to start a chain reaction of everybody looking at *their* watches or phones, for that may distract all of them. Somehow, it stopped. My timer stopped. I just had to continue. I kept going. I could not get distracted by this. I previously prayed for "supernatural time" if it was in His will.

As I spoke, *everybody* remained silent and listened attentively with no distractions whatsoever. Ultimately, I got to say what I rehearsed so long for. Afterwards, everybody there clapped and cheered as loud as thunder for so long. It took a couple of moments to quiet everybody down from clapping so that I could say the prayer. Subsequently, people clapped for a few seconds more before departing.

A friend came up to me and complimented, "That was a-a-awesome."

The person who was in charge of FCA for a few schools in our district gave me a high five. With a big, wide smile, she exclaimed, "You sure know how to preach it, brother!"

However, there was one thing that I did not hear. It was the bell. I then looked down at my wristwatch, and I am not joking with you. I am telling the honest truth. I had five minutes—*five* minutes—to spare!

While this was not the first time public speaking before—and certainly not the last—it was surely a momentous, pivotal day in my life. It is leading me far—even to the fact that you are reading this. For a person who has struggled with several issues of Asperger's syndrome, this has been quite a special opportunity.

In fact, it was not long before I got to speak again. I told the former senior commander at my Royal Rangers outpost about it. He said that he would love to hear it and asked me if I wanted to do five minutes of it in a devotion for the following week. I went straight to the point: when Jesus was born. I continued on from there.

There were two devotions that evening out in the grassland of Newport Mesa Church. I was first. After I finished speaking, with the sun in its first stages of setting, the former senior commander slowly walked over to me. With a closed, pierced-lip smile, he just stared at me for several seconds, then at the rest of the outpost. It took me a moment to figure it out.

"Come on, [commander]! Real men cry!" the commander who was doing the devotion after me hollered out. This confirmed my realization.

The senior commander spoke after a couple more seconds of regrouping and gave me a great commendation in front of everybody. After that, the other commander came up to do his devotion.

"It's very intimidating to be speaking right after Matthew," he started.

It did not end there. In the first weekend of June 2013,

there was an annual pow-wow in Jurupa Valley. Present at this huge, three-day campout were several different outposts of Southern California. (I could only stay for two days, because I had a HALO Benefit show on June 9th that I performed in.) In the evening of the second day, all the outposts went in front of everybody, one by one, to give their outpost skit and outpost yell.

On the way over, the day prior, the former senior commander notified me that my devotion was going to be the majority of the outpost skit. As I delivered my message once more, I was orating in front of a good number of people (boys, their dads, and their commanders). Everybody together probably exceeded the headcount of FCA that day on May 10th.

During our individual outpost camp that October 5th, one of the commanders from the district came by. "Some of us are still talking about that," he complimented me, in reference to my speech. Apparently, I left a big impression.

I suppose that the next step in fulfilling my calling into ministry is being asked by lead pastors to deliver devotions in front of everybody in the main sanctuary at churches on Sunday mornings.

Before I go up to give any message, I always pray that the Holy Spirit would speak through me and help me not to stutter. The next time when I got to deliver my entire message, like how I did at FCA, was at Victory Fellowship OC in August 2015.

There is one more hindrance to public speaking, but I have been greatly successful at overcoming it so far. However, it has not yet entirely disappeared. It is spontaneously becoming distracted, which could provoke stuttering. I have been victorious at containing a great list of things in my memory during public speaking. Still, that is a lot of things to say, and I am determined to finish what I started. Usually, raised hands, interruptions from others, or anything in that nature can make me briefly lose my train of thought. Even the *thought* that I would get cut off is an obstructive interruption.

People may assume that I am overestimating children and confusing them with complicated, college-level diction, mathematics, history, and sciences. However, I am nearly positive that I have edited out most of those things unless I strongly feel that it is pertinent *and* that I can successfully elucidate their definitions in a timely manner. I worry that I would be interrupted by being asked to skip it. They might conclude that I am the one assuming that the children would understand, even though I have not yet even begun to lucidly define what I am talking about.

I do endeavor to make sure that I speak in the vernacular of the age group whom I am talking to, whether I am giving a devotion, teaching a weekly Bible study, or teaching a merit. I am open to questions to answer and clarify. As much as I would love to tutor them in how to take derivatives, apply chain rule, solve by implicit differentiation, and explain what all that calculus means, I am confident that most of them are not ready yet. (I am furthermore strongminded to speak as accurately as I can; I refuse to make up short answers to fill in the gaps.)

Most of the time, nobody cuts me off, and that worry was for nothing, but how could I have been sure? Nevertheless, intrusive distractions—by whatever means or phenomena—do occur, and render me stuttering and having possible apprehension.

I came up with the most quintessential analogy where I use Boyle's Law to illustrate my point. Boyle's Law is one of the simple gas laws. It states that volume and pressure are inversely proportional. That is, when the volume of a gas *decreases*, then pressure *increases* and vice versa (assuming that both the amount of gas and its temperature are held constant).

The time frame that I am given represents the volume (the amount of space or time there is available for me). Whenever any distraction occurs, it takes up a part of the time allotted—thereby decreasing the "volume" of the time for my speech. In accordance with Boyle's Law, when volume decreases, obviously (and intuitively), the pressure increases. Here is the takeaway: Decreasing the volume of time that I have available (to deliver a speech or have a conversation) increases the pressure (i.e., stress) inside. It is the classic fight-or-flight response.

(I can parallel this with running out of time to get somewhere. The decrease in the amount of time that I have to get from point A to point B even when I am running late for being early increases pressure).

Distractions can simply come in the form of a noise from either inside or out. Wherever I am speaking, there are usually some people of all ages who chatter throughout my entire speech, even seconds after starting. Through this experience, it has helped me greatly. It helped me to get prepared, used to it, and to *anticipate* it. Whenever anybody is practicing anything, they need to get ready for potential (and even unforeseeable) distractions and divergences that act as roadblocks to their goals.

And that is the epitome that every Royal Ranger strives for: being *ready* for any possible attack that the devil can throw at us! I have personally fought the devil many times and came out victorious. According to the first point of the Royal Ranger Code, Alert, we need to live by this verse:

> *Be sober, be vigilant; because your adversary the devil, as a roaring lion, walketh about, seeking whom he may devour* (1 Peter 5:8).

Whenever I am trusted and taken into people's confidence to help them out with their schoolwork, questions, or struggles, it is a surreal feeling of success. I am practicing advocacy and responsibility. I am growing up to be the man and leader that God has called me to be.

I always endeavor to have an answer, but I accept that I will still be learning and picking up on new things. Each and every day is a learning experience, and that is another fun part to acknowledge. I have gotten a great start with Royal Rangers.

With all of this said, I aspire to speak in front of bigger and bigger crowds as I strive to continue implementing elocution. I am diminishing my stuttering and boldly starting to begin conversations on my own. I am breaking away from my social shyness and beginning to be my own advocate. Through Royal Rangers, I am becoming a leader and soaring farther beyond what was probable (according to a list of statistics written down in a book about autism somewhere) for a person like me who has a "disability."

25

My Trilogy

For three days in late May 2013, I got to stay home from school because as a senior, I did not have to take the annual STAR Test. I decided to have a verse-by-verse Bible study with my grandfather and a friend of ours; our friend is a pastor. For each of the three days, we studied Obadiah, Philemon, and Titus, respectively. For the next few years, we went through most of the New Testament, the Minor Prophets, and a few more books of the Old Testament. All of these treasured memories had been quite beneficial. I received superb understanding and insight.

I understood a lot of the details that are mentioned in Daniel 2, 7, and 8, as well as the Book of Revelation (which is one of my many favorite books, along with Daniel). I had been curious as to what several of the Minor Prophets are about, like Habakkuk, for we do not seem to hear much about them as often as we probably should.

I have used a plethora of the themes and messages from these books and incorporated them into my devotions for Royal Rangers. I have already had an understanding of the Bible's timeline and got extremely interested in biblical chronology since I was at least thirteen or fourteen. I have made charts, timelines, and done my own mathematics and research in the process.

These Bible studies crucially helped magnify my comprehension of Scripture, yet there are several, several things that I still do not know. I am always going to learn more, even after reading through Bible books ten times over. One vital thing that I have learned is to accept that I can neither find every single detail that I search for, nor ever be able to answer *every* question asked—especially the hairsplitting ones. And *those answers* are the ones that I always want to know.

> *The secret things belong unto the LORD our God: but those things which are revealed belong unto us and to our children for ever* (Deuteronomy 29:29).

Simply, God did not reveal everything. In fact, we cannot even live if we knew everything—it would be too much. I never intend to reach such an impossible goal. What He did reveal to us is simply what is important for us to know. Likewise, He does not reveal His plan for our lives all at once. We put it together piece by piece along our walk with God. I personally know some of the things that He calls me to, but the *entire* plan has not yet been revealed.

Soon, I acquired the zeal to take what I learned about the Bible, use Scripture verses, and write short essays about it. For instance, one on Daniel 2, 7, and 8. One on sin and grace, one on love, one on idolatry, and one on eschatology.

Suddenly, it came to me probably in September 2013. I envisioned myself writing a series of fictional short stories that were entirely based on my devotions/essays. I thought, *What shall I name my main character?* "Habakkuk" *instantly* came to mind. Habakkuk? I put that on the shelf and waited to see if it would become pertinent later on.

Now, I am an extremely creative writer. I have been coming up with fictional stories all my life—even in middle and high school. It is super easy to come up with allegories as well. I persevered to never give up on these short stories. In the early fall of 2013, I sat down in front of my laptop and began the opening paragraph. I started with an introductory behind the characters and where they lived. I decided to have my main character—whom I ended up naming Habakkuk after all—to be born on my birthday, July 22nd, but in the year 1950 (45 years before I was born). I chose to have the family live in the rural 1950s, in northern Louisiana. Thus, I would get to write about a time and place where I felt like I grew up in, even though I was born in the middle of the 1990s and raised mostly in the city.

I had only been to Texas once for my first Mother's Day in 1996, so it is safe to assume that I do not remember it at all. Other than that, I always stayed in California. In fact, if it were not for my grandfather joining the United States Navy at age seventeen to support his family, then he would not have moved to California and met his wife. Thus, none of my family would probably be living here right now in California. I have found this to be a gigantic blessing for my life. Who knows where I would be today?

Hardly stopping, I just typed on and on and on. It was one of my favorite projects. I could not wait for the free time to get back to it again. It was relaxing, and I was passionate about it.

Since it is enormously difficult for me to stop something once I start it, I just kept on going. Soon, I had to force myself to shut the computer down for the night, only to stay awake as I visualized where I was at in the storyline. I often wrote the next couple of stories down in my mind. I just cannot help it. Additionally, I was in my first semester of college at the same time, but the homework was super easy, and I always found plenty of free time. Pretty soon, this first short story became longer and eventually turned into a novella. Ultimately, I decided to make this into a novel, combining all of my devotions, with the finale paralleling my speech from May 10th.

Furthermore, I decided to make Habakkuk be diagnosed with Asperger's syndrome too. That way, through him, I could articulate the many issues that we face and the several gifts with which we are personally awarded. Therefore, Habakkuk is characteristically inquisitive. Likewise, the Prophet Habakkuk asked questions that he did not understand during his complaining to the Lord.

I have made tons of parallel stories between Habakkuk's life and my life. (Not exact parallels but *based* on them.) I started thinking hard about the title. After a while, I came up with the quintessential one: *Witnessing Habakkuk.*

The title, *Witnessing Habakkuk*, has three meaning:

> People witness others like witnessing historical events. In this book, the readers are seeing this boy, Habakkuk, as he lives his childhood and teenage years.
>
> *Witnessing Habakkuk* becomes this boy's title, because he likes to witness/evangelize, whereas "witnessing" in this context is the present participle (an adjective) in this form.
>
> Finally, he is *Witnessing Habakkuk* with "witnessing" being the present participle again, because he is the one witnessing events in both history and in his personal life—being the observant, close-to-detail individual that he is.

I began hoping that this book could reach out to many people and families of what exactly Asperger's is like, encompassing what we go through, as well as the amazing aspects of it. I feel that this can further make people aware of what this reality is. Also, I wanted it to be in the form of a fictional novel.

> *Although the fig tree shall not blossom, neither shall fruit be in the vines; the labour of the olive shall fail, and the fields shall yield no meat; the flock shall be cut off from the fold, and there shall be no herd in the stalls: Yet I will rejoice in the Lord, I will joy in the God of my salvation* (Habakkuk 3:17-18).

Habakkuk 3:17-18 is personally one of my favorite passages in the Bible, and I feel that it is unassailably suitable. In the novel, Habakkuk witnesses lots of things, both bad and good. The readers witness him as he experiences and copes with trials in his own life and in his family as they deal with the events that went on in their home, their country, and the world at the time.

Yet! We shall remember Jesus, what He has done for us, that He is in control, and that everything will be okay. We shall continue to *rejoice* in Him. He is returning soon. And soon, there will be a day when He will set up His earthly kingdom.

Near the end of October 2013, I had completed my first draft. As time went on, I had a few people read it and received positive reviews. Over the next few years, I had gone through the entire manuscript several times and essentially dwarfed my first final draft. Saying that I am merely dedicated to this novel is a boulder-sized understatement. This novel has seemingly become one of the ultra-main focuses that I constantly thought about—day and night. I had invested quite a bit of energy and tens of thousands of hours of planning and writing.

Throughout the entire timespan of authoring this novel, I scrupulously jotted notes down on several pieces of paper. I always kept folded pieces of paper and Post-It Notes ready in my pocket. It did not matter where I was at, or what I was doing. No joke, but I literally had to tape a few pages (one page at a time) on the wall next to my bed, because I *always* kept getting new ideas in the middle of the night. I kept a marker on the desk next to me. Whenever I had gotten an idea, I would just mark on the piece of paper on the wall, even while it was relatively dark.

The most memorable part of this entire process was collecting my ideas while hiking around the neighborhood. Neighborhood hikes are cathartic for me, as I get to tranquilly think, regroup, and/or rehearse. In evening walks, skies start to redden due to the setting sun, and the trees and houses begin to turn into a silhouette. The breeze blows around me, and the birds sing their choruses. I enjoy nature. It makes me jubilant and infests me with goosebumps. It evokes my childhood, and that is exactly part of what I want to convey through my novel.

I put detailed imagery throughout the novel, and I hope that the reader can grasp how I personally view the serene outdoors. Each of the four seasons and each of the twelve months has a distinguishable mood to me when it comes to conditions like the atmosphere, temperature, and climate. (It is like I can breathe differently in autumn than in summer, for example.) When I would write a side story on the laptop that I rehearsed in my head during a walk, I could recall exactly where I was at during the walk.

By spring 2016, it was time to make a choice. With prayer, I browsed throughout the internet for a Christian literary agent. I prayed that it would be someone who might be able to find the quintessential publisher. I hoped and prayed that the novel would greatly help several people around the world, as I believe it will, and lead me to several churches, schools, community centers to help people. I finally found one whom I believed would be perfect. I contacted him and sent him my manuscript. In June 2016, we had, I would say, a powerful consultation call for roughly ninety minutes. If it were not for this conversation, you probably would not be reading this right now.

Intrinsically, I always have written more than what was required. The agent first said that my novel would be over four and five hundred pages long. I was personally not surprised. In fact, that was one of the main things that I was concerned about. He then complimented me by saying, "You do have an ability to write and articulate your thought." Later on, he reopened my original thought of writing short stories. He liked that idea.

Ultimately, words cannot express the gratitude of being able to talk with him about my project. I consider it as God leading me to him. In the end, I got encouraged to simply write an anthology of autobiographical short stories, based on real-life experiences of having Asperger's, in addition to sharing how God has been helping me through it. I literally do not know where I would be now without publishing this book first, for I can still publish the novel sometime hereafter.

I have been debating and debating and debating and debating on whether or not to break up my huge novel into a trilogy of three smaller novels. Will it be more beneficial? What if people do not like the first one? I was still quite concerned about its formidable size. There were a couple of outstanding pros and cons that I am sure every author faces.

After asking a few people (including a couple of authors whom I know), in December 2016, I officially declared that my novel would be a trilogy. I felt that would be best. By late spring 2017, I have accomplished this.

I can testify that each time an author goes through their work, it gets better and better each time. I have gone through this project cover-to-cover several times since its inception in 2013.

In summary, it has been almost six years since I officially

started on this journey toward authorship, as of publishing this anthology.

Writing *Witnessing Habakkuk* has been quite an experience. I put together and maximized a lifetime of creative-writing passions and learning. Whenever I had free time, I worked day and night for weeks and months. It was challenging to say "Good night" to it, as I kept working till late at night, night after night. I could not stop until I finished, but I knew that it was impossible to suddenly be done with it right away. Plus, it would be too impetuous. I surmise that it is the perfect amalgamation of excitement, adrenaline, and dedication.

If I had a hundred-dollar bill for every hour I spent writing, rereading, preparing, thinking, researching, and jotting down notes, then I would be a millionaire. And that is a true story! Having Asperger's syndrome, I inherently put an immense wealth of detail down to a science in this trilogy, making sure that everything is mathematically, scientifically, and historically accurate. I researched all around the internet and books in my home library, as well as personal interviews.

Through having both a *fictional trilogy* and a *nonfictional anthology*, readers can read about the issues of Asperger's syndrome and autism with *two* different approaches, yet both have the same overall premises. Based upon preference, readers can choose to read either…or both. If you read this one first and then the trilogy, some of the stories will be familiar, but the trilogy will have a lot more paralleling details to the stories that I did not have space here to say. Plus new stories.

The important thing to note is that I was refreshed and even *learned* in the process (and that is an important acknowledgment). I learned and relearned things from the Bible, vocabulary, grammar, history, science, and various other branches of knowledge. I implemented archetypes and allegorical writing, which is something I started practicing since at least high school. It evoked a myriad of benevolent family memories, as well as other cordial reminisces, but it nonetheless revived the hard, not-so-good times.

I am thankful for this talent that God has given me, and I strongly feel that this is a part of what is in His plan from my life. Having autism and Asperger's can sadden families and slow them down, but I know that God has chosen me to have this condition, so that I may be one of the few who could encourage and reassure others. This is just one of several things that I feel He is calling me to do.

26

ART

I thoroughly enjoy the carefreeness of moving a pencil while detailing nature scenes, the soothing back and forth motion of the hand when shading in a portrait, and the serenity of escaping the burdens and problems of life to spend a few hours drawing or painting.

Art is another talent that God has given me. All my life, I loved drawing, coloring, and painting. As far back as I can remember, I would draw and color. From crayons to chalk to paint, art is something that is quite calming and makes me feel tranquil.

Art is just like creative writing. Once I start, it is hard for me to stop since I intend to finish what I start. We did a myriad of art projects throughout elementary school. Assign me a simple stick-figure project, and I could give you Rembrandt or M.C. Escher (okay, well I am not *that* good, but relatively speaking). Obviously, I go overboard. With Asperger's, like lots of people with it, I am very attentive to detail and precision.

In fourth grade, I would doodle throughout my composition book and draw the front cover of storybooks. Quite a few times, drawing in class instead of listening to the teacher or working on projects has almost gotten me into big trouble. The closer I was to finishing, the more frustrating it became when I was caught.

Drawing is cathartic. It taught me patience, as some art projects required days. It is a release of various pressures that I may be facing. It is like putting together a jigsaw puzzle or solving some big algebra, trigonometry, calculus, or chemistry problem.

As a Discovery Ranger in Royal Rangers, I unsurprisingly earned the Art merit. It always elated me when my friends got to see what I could do. I enjoyed hearing "Whoa" and "That's really good." It kept me motivated. It made me feel that there is one more thing I can do and do for others.

Around nine, ten, and eleven years old, I would watch various art and painting shows, including Bob Ross' *The Joy of Painting* and *Pappyland.* I persistently pretended that I had such an art show too. I must have drawn tens of thousands of pictures in my life so far. I wouldn't be surprised. Just like creative writing, I have added hidden messages, symbols, and microprinting in some of my drawings, some of which I have learned in Art History class during freshman year.

An older friend of mine from church would have cell group at his trailer park's clubhouse and later, in his trailer. One Thursday night at the clubhouse when I was ten, my grandfather called me over, saying, "You aren't the only artist here." From a distance, I thought the man in the wheelchair was drawing Lady Liberty from the Walker Half Dollar, but when I got closer, it was actually Popeye. From that night until he passed away in 2014, he has really helped me out in my passion for art through techniques and materials, such as paints, pastels, sketchbooks, and art kits.

To no surprise, I maintained being an artist throughout middle and high school. I took a semester of art in seventh grade and a year of art in eighth as electives at Ensign Intermediate. In these classes, we learned incalculable techniques in art, including pointillism, one-point perspective, two-point perspective, and much more. It was not just drawing and painting, but we made crafts, such as thoroughly putting together our own sketchbooks, making masks of ourselves, and carving rubber stamps that we got to utilize. I additionally learned how to mix colors to make flesh tones.

Having Asperger's, I characteristically always strived to make the most complicated-looking, time-consuming projects. To this day, I aspire to be the most creative and fastidious in detail. A few of my projects were based on presidents, history, and national landmarks.

For most of my artwork, it became hard for some people to believe that I drew it freehand. Even my own grandfather questioned me a few times. I entered many art contests on my own and sometimes got an honorable mention.

Before school started one foggy morning in eighth grade, I was picking up the mail in the front office for my first-period teacher and talking to a friend of mine. The principal came out of his office and said that he had a surprise for me. He took me over to the "beehive" (at Ensign, we were the Seabees) where there were stacks and stacks of directories. He held one of them up with a big, broad smile and on the cover was my mural submission! I became jubilant. Apparently, it was the number-one choice that they decided to put on the front of the directory too.

The other six contestants and I drew and painted the murals in March 2009 by the cafeteria. It took between seven and eight total hours for me to complete. This became a huge blessing and a cherished memory. The next morning on the way to church, I suddenly remembered that I forgot to paint the stars in the flag. Being persnickety, I called the head coordinator, and that afternoon, he came by with white paint.

I visited the murals from time to time until 2015. Then one day, in December, the wall was completely white. All seven murals from 2009 were painted over. It was not a dream.

Apparently, there was vandalism, and they had to paint it over. Now, it only exists in history and the yearbook.

Some artwork and school projects of mine have been lost or thrown away. In seventh grade, I painted William the Conqueror for a project in Foreign Language class. I went overboard again, unsurprisingly. I showed it to my R.S.P. teacher on the morning it was due. A friend of hers was there too, and she said, "This puts Picasso to shame!" It was on display by the library until September 2008. Unfortunately, it had most likely been thrown away.

That happens. Inevitably, I cannot undo the fact that something has been damaged or lost. Whether I redo the project in its entirety or restore it, it still can never be the original. It is analogous to cleaning and polishing an old coin, which could severely lower its value.

In freshman year over at Newport Harbor High, I took Art History. The first and third semester was art ,and the second and fourth was the history of art. In May 2010, I got second place in the school's art fair. Just like at Ensign, I chose to do artworks pertaining to history and historical figures, specifically Abraham Lincoln.

In sophomore year, one of my best homework submissions for Honors Biology was a detailed drawing and coloring of the anatomy of a tarantula. My former art teacher let me borrow watercolor pencils, and after coloring, I added water to turn it into paint.

For this project, I had chosen to go overboard with time-consuming, realistic details again because other students were complaining about how impossible it looked to draw. And in my dictionary, the word "impossible" is rarely used. Moans signal me to spend extra time on such assignments, for I like choosing the formidable-looking diagrams.

In junior year, God had me meet a friend at St. Andrew's Presbyterian, who is also a talented artist. He gave me helpful ideas, including how to draw and color portraits of people. I spent the next several months drawing all the presidents in this technique. Each portrait took a few hours.

In my senior year, I chose to take anatomy, and we had tons and tons of drawing and labeling to do in nearly every single chapter.

I drew the different types of tissues in chapter four, the skin and hair follicles in chapter five, but my teacher was most astounded in January 2013. I turned in my pencil sketches of the six synovial joints from chapter seven, the arthrology chapter. Apparently, it must have looked incredibly real to everybody whom I showed it to, including a couple of friends at the school library while I was in the middle of drawing those diagrams. I showed them to a friend of mine after it was completed, and she told me, "I cannot believe that you drew this. I mean, I believe you because you told me, but…I still cannot believe it."

Within days after turning it in, my anatomy teacher told me that he showed the diagrams to his family and friends. He told me that one of his friends said, "He is really good with computer art."

Then my teacher told his friend, "No! My student actually drew this by hand." He said that his friend took a closer look and said, "If he seriously loves doing this, he should *really* consider being a medical artist for textbooks."

In my opinion, the culmination came on February 26-27, 2013. On these two days, I drew four diagrams of the human heart that were assigned. Once again, it was detailed. Like the tarantula, I colored it with watercolor pencils and added water to turn it into paint.

"If you like to draw—" one of the leaders at the high school youth group of St. Andrew's Presbyterian Church began. It was toward the end of a Christmas party in December 2011.

In that picosecond, I was alert and ready to inquire what the project was. My ears heard loud and clear. It was to read a chapter from *The Story* and either draw or paint a picture of what I read. I accepted the project and took the book home, along with a small canvas. I read chapter 23 about Jesus. After planning and painting, I presented it on New Year's, 2012. It had been a very fun, rewarding, and memorable project. The entire church went through *The Story* sermon series, based on the book, from January to June 2012, which summarizes the entire Bible.

In January 2012, the same leader again asked if anyone would like to read a chapter and take a canvas home. This time, many more volunteered. I asked if I could do another one. She said it was okay and told me to read chapter 29, which was much longer. It was all about the Apostle Paul.

This time, I chose a canvas that was four feet long and two feet wide. It took a *lot* of planning, a *long* time drawing it, and a *long* time painting it. Before I finished painting it, I took it to Royal Rangers to share with the Adventure and Expedition Rangers. Everybody's artwork was displayed where the high school youth group worshipped and listened to the weekly message.

When we got toward chapter 23 in the series, I was filmed talking about my painting and the messages inside it. I was very excited to talk about chapter 29. They said I could, but out of nowhere, they were on chapter 29, so I never got to talk about it.

Looking back at my artwork, I can see that it is usually attached to a memory. I could remember where I was when I drew or painted it, and the surroundings. I could recall whether or not

I was listening to music or watching something on the T.V. set. Now and again, if I listen to the same music or watch the same show or movie, it evokes the artwork.

For instance, while painting about the missions and writings of the Apostle Paul, which took several days, the original *The Adventures of Spin and Marty* (a 1950s series by *The Mickey Mouse Club*) was on the television set. We got the DVD from our local library. It was just something to have on in the background. They constantly sang a theme song about the Triple R, and I would have episode after episode play back to back. (Hard to explain, music helps motivate me as I work on projects and mathematics.) Now, whenever I think about painting it, I can easily hear the song played in my mind and vice versa.

I have drawn, colored, and painted all my life, and I still do so today. It has always been one of my favorite, relaxing pastimes. God has blessed me with this talent of being an artist. I am thankful for the compliments, recognition, and awards that I have received. It reminds me of all the benevolent, supporting friends that I have and the cordial events that I have attended.

27

ENTREPRENEURSHIP

Before the advent of high school, I officially launched "Matthew Cards" at age thirteen. Realizing that a lot of entrepreneurs name their businesses by their last names, I immediately changed it to "Kenslow Cards" shortly afterward. Kenslow Cards is a self-employed, sole-proprietor card company with which the Lord has blessed me.

A lifelong friend of mine has a granddaughter who started making and selling cards herself. This friend has also been a gigantic supporter in my artwork for several years. She figured that designing cards would be a great job for me. She sent me money for supplies, and on that sunny summer day, I initiated the business.

I sold my first card on Monday, December 21, 2009, and have since produced lots of designs. Since drawing and coloring are cathartic, I always enjoyed creating the picturesque nature scenes and wildlife. Now and again, I spontaneously added new things to the artwork when I was in the middle of drawing it. It was sort of like what Bob Ross would do.

A few ideas for designs were inspired by people who would order them. Other ideas were from those asking if I had a design for a particular occasion (such as a retirement, a season, or a holiday).

Then there were designs completely inspired by real events. For instance, my camping design (which features a traditional campout scene, a lake, a forest of trees in the background, and the rising of a full moon behind them) was directly inspired by a Royal Rangers campout at Lake Hemet from April 2013. I drew about ninety-nine percent of it from memory. When one of my commanders saw it, he showed it to everyone. One of the Expedition Rangers and future-GMA recipient complimented me by saying, "You're better than my art teacher."

My vacation design (which features a sailing, triple-decker yacht in the foreground of an island) was inspired by my round trip to Catalina the day I turned eighteen.

My Christmas 2014 design, which I completed in early September, was inspired by a message at Newport Mesa Church during their annual Christmas Tree Blessing night.

In early December 2013, one of my former commanders from Royal Rangers had given the message. He had one of the several Christmas trees by him; these trees were going to be taken to people's homes that night. There were two other people with Christmas trees next to him, one on both sides. At the culmination of the message, all three of them raised their Christmas trees up on their shoulders. The three stands faced the audience, which portrayed the three crosses. The reason why Jesus had been born was to go to the cross to wash away our innate, inescapable sin.

Both the commander and I had the same exact idea: make that into a card. Therefore, I did.

On the design, I drew three people, each holding a Christmas tree on their shoulder, presenting it like the three crosses. They were in front of an open door, standing at the end of a long, windy path that led from the stable with a manger in it. A great light shone down from the night sky directly over the stable. On both sides of the lit stable were the silhouettes of skyscrapers.

The encompassing stars were all shaped like crosses. And guess where I got that from. No joke, but that was inspired by a real dream I had in August 2014. How I remember it, I was coming back home at night somewhere past E. 17th Street. I looked up at the clear sky looking southwest, and I saw a myriad of white, twinkling crosses as stars, slowly moving from east to west.

With all the detail that I put into this, I certainly could not have done it through the method that I had originally intended.

Initially, back in 2009, I planned to design cards, assemble them, and sell them, but after that, I started keeping one card of each design and placing them all in a portfolio. From there, I started taking orders through special alphanumeric codes (for example, KC3 meant Kenslow Cards design #3; KCP1 denoted Kenslow Cards Pop-up design #1). Upon receiving an order, I would draw the design from scratch. That did not last long since it would take a long time to mass produce. Ultimately, after a couple of amendments, and since I got much more artistic and detailed with my designs, I kept a colorized master to copy from.

By November of 2012, I had made my one-thousandth dollar. As 2013 dawned, I started getting even faster in assembling cards. On February 19th, I bought a paper cutter that can cut with crazy cuts; I also started printing my designs on shipping labels. I tested it out two days later, and it worked perfectly. Now, with the shipping labels, all I have to do is peel off the back and paste them onto the cardstock.

I determined that this does save time. I always hand drew my logo on the back, but in May, I purchased two stamps—one for the logo and the other for the tagline, which gives details about the company. On most of the cards, I still place my signature by hand.

Kenslow Cards soon became a profitable business. I had previously started filling out sales orders in December 2011 and created a Facebook page in August of the next year. Through this, I felt like a real businessman and had started to implement responsibility and advocacy, which is an important experience for those with Asperger's syndrome and autism. For me, I found it through Kenslow Cards. Others found it through other means like part-time jobs around the community.

Having this company helped me in two of my high school classes at Newport Harbor, plus my Senior Exit Project. The first class was in Multi-Media International Business in junior year, and the second was in Economics class in senior year. Both projects required us to create a business, but I already had a real one. Both teachers said that it was okay. For our project in Economics class, we had to build our own website, and that is how Kenslow Cards officially got a website toward the middle of December 2012.

Alas and quite disconcerting, the company that I would buy the cardstock from suddenly stopped selling it. This happened once before with another brand, but we found this particular brand soon after. We could not yet find anything that would perfectly suffice. Thus, Kenslow Cards has been on a temporary (hopefully) hiatus for nearly a few years now.

I kept detailed records of all the basics mainly by hand: who ordered what design, the date, the amount, the revenue (weekly, monthly, and yearly), the expenses (monthly and yearly), the profits, the ROI, and graphs. I kept and compiled my receipts in order.

In summary, Kenslow Cards has been much more than a business to earn money. Kenslow Cards has exceptionally helped me in employing salesmanship and responsibility. (In 2013, I earned the Salesmanship merit at Royal Rangers.) I utilized resources and made solo trips to stores for copies and supplies. I designed and assembled cards while using my original artwork and figured out the best way for me to mass produce cards quicker and quicker. I sociably went up to people to ask them if they needed to buy cards.

It has unequivocally been a blessing and a great implementation for advocacy.

28

SHARING IDEAS

All of us probably grew up doing thousands of group projects in school. Just like my innate trait to control a conversation, I had characteristically endeavored to dominate a project. It is most often hard to collaborate ideas, and naturally, I felt that mine were the best, just like the students with whom I was working. If they disagreed, then I would argue with them. I persevered to have the best project, and if it was a *group* project, I strived to have my entire group be the number-one project even when there was not a competition. Nevertheless, part of having an outstanding group project is the conglomeration of the ideas of *every* member.

In music class at Newport Heights Elementary, however, we once had to compose a few measures of music with a partner. I recall having my own melody in mind. Next thing I knew, my friend told the music teacher and got into another group.

When I am working on a group project, I take it as working independently on homework. The only times when I am thankful for a group project is when I have entirely no clue what the project is about. Thus, if needed, I contribute by doing the artwork.

Part of the reason why I did not always convey some of my inventive ideas to the group that much is the nervousness of hearing "No," "It'll be too hard," "It won't work," or "You're doing it the hard way." I heard those comments often, yet they just motivated me to try harder. I like to *prove* that something is doable and that I could do it, which has occurred. I could take my idea home, work hours on it, and come back with it.

In sophomore year, I did ninety-nine percent of the work on a creative writing project for World History class regarding the French Revolution, and practically the entire PowerPoint presentation regarding Cuba. Likewise, in senior year, there were at least two other PowerPoint projects where I did most of the slides. It is not so much that my partners did not do anything, it was how I inherently cannot seem to realize how working together *could* work smoothly; I cannot seem to function that way. Being fastidious to micro-detail, I must have felt that working on something together might deteriorate the overall effect. On the contrary, I probably had that backward, but Asperger's tricks me otherwise. I have put in a tremendous amount of effects and enhancements that were not all required in my numerous PowerPoint and creative writing projects.

Like I said toward the beginning, I liked group projects when I hardly knew the material. However, when the teacher told us to get into groups ourselves, that usually aggravated me. I disliked it. *We* had to pick our partners. I quickly started to count everybody in the classroom, and almost always—almost always—it was an odd number. That meant that I had to find a friend, pronto!

Contrariwise, there had been several times when the teacher said, "Get into groups," and a friend asked me if I wanted to be their partner. Once in a blue moon, I got the privilege to have been asked by a couple of students. Nonetheless, that apprehended me all the same. I was faced with choosing one out of two or three friends. If I chose the wrong one, the other might be disappointed; conversely, if I chose the right one, the other would be okay with it and find someone else.

Having Asperger's syndrome, I guess I am nervous about disheartening others inadvertently, and it is also challenging to collaborate ideas. It inherently still is sometimes. That must be the introverted side of me.

I learned to share ideas as I grew older since that is good teamwork.

I start to feel selfish when I do not take the time to listen to another person's ideas. It might as well be an independent assignment, where I have the liberty to do one-hundred percent of the work. I try to make sure nowadays that others have a say in the group project. Importantly, it is great to share ideas because a few heads are definitely better than one.

29

The Laughter of Slapstick Comedy…Oh, Wait

There goes Charlie Chaplain! There goes Moe, Larry, and Curly! There goes Tom chasing Jerry! I watched all these characters on television. I laughed—which was intended by the makers of the shows. Nevertheless, one scene in a hundred could be quite disturbing to me. This statistic applies to several of the contemporary kids shows that my generation grew up with as they became more violent. Some of my friends and schoolmates would emulate them. That is why some of them left a formidable impression on me.

One of my friends at Newport Heights Elementary got upset at another mutual friend ruining his game on his PalmPilot. I overheard him telling other friends that he was going to take this mutual friend after school and "bang his head against the wall until it breaks."

People laughed about it then, and people may laugh about it now, but please consider that it is a human life. Each person has only one life. If any irreparable damage incurs, that person might die or become a quadriplegic. They may never talk, see, or hear again. Life is not a videogame where everything can start over when there are multiple "*lives*." Life is neither a movie where the tape can be rewound and started over, nor a fairytale with magic and special potions that can remarkably cure anything, even death.

I started to routinely look over my shoulder to make sure that I had a way to escape. I located where the nearest teachers and lunch aides were at. Additionally, there were a couple of students who picked on me just because I was different.

With Asperger's, I can inherently interpret a lot of things in the world quite differently. All my life, when things are funny to other people, they may not be funny to me. Contrastingly, when things are funny to me, they may not be funny to others. I laugh and tell jokes, especially starting in fifth grade. In retrospect, it may have been a catharsis to placate certain individual students. I started picking up on past mistakes, acquired better sportsmanship, and became nicer than I was already.

I once laughed myself out a dream…literally. Back in elementary school, I had a dream where my R.S.P. teacher made such a funny face that I started laughing (in and out of the dream), which woke me up…and my mother.

I undergo "laugh spasms," as I call them, when I cannot stop laughing for a million dollars. With tears flowing down my face, it could last for a long time. With my impediment, I can hardly enunciate anything when I laugh that hard. Others laugh not because they understand what is funny to me, but because I am laughing.

I believe what I read in the Scriptures, when it says:

> *A merry heart maketh a cheerful countenance: but by sorrow of the heart the spirit is broken* (Proverbs 15:13).

> *A merry heart doeth good like a medicine: but a broken spirit drieth the bones* (Proverbs 17:22).

Whenever I cannot help but laugh, I am still conscious of the people around me. I never want to inadvertently offend them by laughing. Since a boy, I have had to learn the difference between reality and slapstick comedy. When people are hurt, it is no laughing matter. I had trained myself not to laugh. Sometimes, it is irrepressible (partly due to Asperger's). In that case, I try extra hard to hide it.

To reiterate, there are things funny to others but not funny to me. One of the quintessential examples of this occurred in fifth grade. Unbeknownst to him, my teacher used a tragicomic example for something that he was teaching us.

Let us say that a mother promised her son that she would take him to the park after school. The son looked forward to it all day, but when he got home, the mother told him that his little sister was sick. Accordingly, the son could not go to the park that day. Rather, the next day. What should the son do? Basically, our teacher was telling us that we are supposed to accept it and say, "Okay." Then, while acting it out, our teacher said something like, "It *wouldn't* be okay if he took a chair and started throwing it all around the house."

At that moment, I joined the entire class in an uproar of laughter, but suddenly I was jolted with emotion. For one beat, my heart felt like it would rip out of my chest. One nanosecond, I was laughing. The next, I was seemingly disquieted.

That's sad! I thought to myself. *To be excited all day for something, but then it doesn't happen. But that's not entirely what is sad. What is distressing is the hypothetical of being so broken that you would destroy household objects and throw them around.*

I have helplessly had "sad thoughts" (as I call them) throughout my life. They are mainly wild hypotheticals but are definitely probable if people are not careful. Having Asperger's, I cannot seem to stop them from infiltrating into my mind. I guess it is innate. To make it worse, about ninety-nine percent of my friends would not give it a second thought. Intrinsically, I guess I tend to make mountains out of molehills.

Hypothetically speaking, what if somebody dropped an expensive meal or dessert after paying money for it? (And for many people, unfortunately, five dollars is costly.)

My mother told me a story back when I was around ten or eleven. When she was in high school, a man in the parking lot of the Golden Pheasant restaurant in Torrance asked her if she had money for something to eat, so she gave him some money. When they were driving away, she saw him through the passenger window, eating his hot dog. To my mother, that was a sad moment, because the man did not have money to buy himself something to eat. Hearing the story that happened almost a couple of decades before I was born, I totally empathized with that man. We are not sure if he is still alive.

Time limits have always been stressful for me. What if somebody was rewarded an hour of free time (let us say from class or work), but panicked because they wanted to have the most fun and relaxing time that they possibly could. Then afterward, a list of things to do to relax finally came to mind.

What if a luxurious computer, antique, or chandelier was just procured after years of saving money for it, and it fell and shattered? Or what if an earthquake or flood destroyed it?

Worse, what if it was a priceless, one-of-a-kind, family heirloom passed down for a couple of centuries? (For me, something priceless could be a stack of pictures, original artwork, all of my schoolwork, and even pens and pencils.)

What if a surprise party did not turn out as planned?

What if someone spent a fortune to make somebody happy (even in secrecy), but they did not appreciate the gifts?

What if somebody turned left instead of right on the hiking trail, and something irreversible happened?

What if somebody spent nonrefundable money for something, and it was not what they thought it was? What if it was a book or movie, and it gave them anxiety? What if it was an expensive collectible and it got damaged, broken, lost, or stolen? Then that money had been wasted.

What if a grown, strong-looking man started crying and childishly threw stuff around?

What if a teenager from a poor family worked hard all life long to get a high school diploma, but the cap and gown were too expensive? Let us say they somehow procured one, but it got ripped and ruined right before he walked down the aisle. Or worse, what if he got into a terrible traffic collision right before graduation, and it rendered him quadriplegia?

What if I see people looking sad and eating alone? Are they just on their break from work, and that is how they always look? Or are they homeless, depressed, or lonely, trying to eat their meal?

What if a person bought something like a big pizza for the family or a cup of coffee, and it dropped? What if it happened when they just returned home after traveling many miles for it? What if that person did not drop it and brought it home safely, but the family had prepared something else as a surprise?

What if this happens? What if that happens? This is merely a sample of them. And it gets more heart-wrenching…

Let us say that a young child works hard—doing chores around the house, mowing the neighbor's lawn—to buy a pet. What would happen if the pet ran away? What if it fiercely attacked the child? What if it got hit by a car? The child just worked a year or two for it (hypothetically speaking).

And it does not necessarily have to be a pet. What if the child was saving for a day at the amusement park, but after he got inside, it started to rain and pour? What if the roller coaster decided to derail that day? What if he was saving for an expensive coin for his collection, but it got lost, stolen, or damaged? It is usually harder to deal with a distraught child and not get sad yourself. (As a Royal Rangers commander and even before that, I have dealt with crying children. It may not always be easy but is definitely doable.)

Let us say that a man spends years or a decade looking for a perfect, future wife and finally finds one. Then it takes years, time, effort, and a fortune before they can finally get married. After the marriage, they are at the happiest time in their lives; they waited years for it. But what if immediately afterward, one of them crosses the road and gets killed by a vehicle? The saddest, most painful thing for me, is someone injured or killed when it could have been prevented. Things like these *do* happen in real life, and I came to realize it at an extremely young age. In fact, it probably first started to manifest when I was about six, and it is entirely because of Asperger's.

I always used to get more emotional when it came to babies. They and their parents look very happy and are always smiling. I would hate for something to happen to the baby, considering how fragile and prone to irreparable accidents they could be.

I have personally witnessed people hurt while attending Newport Heights Elementary. In one of those cases, I saw a student trip and fall on the blacktop. Scores of fellow schoolmates came sprinting over and surrounding her. The girl, who later became my friend in high school, was sobbing. I do not recall *anybody* laughing, much less smiling. In fact, and I am not joking, I literally almost teared up seeing her like that, even right now in retrospect. Being that young, I just did not know what to do, so I just helplessly stood there.

This is merely a list of examples. And where did I get some of these from? From television shows, movies, real-life experiences, and even song lyrics. And why do I still have these stuck in my mind since probably preschool? How is it that I cannot forget them? Because of Asperger's! Additionally, my mind can take a happy scene and imagine what could have alternatively happened.

My friends may laugh at such kids' shows because the creators animated the characters in such a way, but I can be disturbed for weeks and months over certain parts. And there is not anything that I can seemingly do about it. Since it is hard for me to forget details, the sad parts just will not go away. Jokes, television shows, and movies can definitely *be* funny, but if some of the scenarios happened in real life to real people, then they could not possibly survive. Each person only has *one* life, yet the characters on these programs and videogames are practically immortal.

In real life, people cannot start over. You do not have to be in a warzone. I feel as if somebody has been mean to me, yelled at me, or betrayed me. Accordingly, my appetite is lost due to the swallowing of disconsolate consternation. I can watch many more things today without any problem, but back then, it was a different story; other things, I usually stay away from.

Apparently, *real* injury cases (whether big or small) can simulate the effects of slapstick comedy. When I was in eighth grade, during physical education class, a basketball hit me right on the top of my head. It was not too hard of a hit, but everybody started laughing out loud instead of helping and caring. Only one person came over to ask if I was alright. Only *one*. That is egregious!

I believe it was in that same year when someone kicked a soccer ball during lunch and at full speed, it hit the head of one of my friends. People started smiling and cracking up. He was alright, but it was a much harder hit. Furthermore, he got very mad about it.

A century or two ago, it would probably not be like that, but how can I be certain? I did not live back in those times. Assuming that I am correct, I theorize that the shows made for children and teenagers nowadays—along with videogames and such—have simulated painful experiences as something humorous. I should know because I grew up watching those shows.

With all of this said, I am now under the impression that if something had happened to me back in school, then everybody would rush over, surround me, stare, point, laugh, and do everything else but help. Contrariwise, if the bullies were the ones who needed serious help, people would view that as the tables turning, but I would still help them regardless in the best way I could. I was certified as an Emergency Medical Responder at age sixteen. I would not want money or gifts in return. Just an apology would suffice—a simple apology to me and all the people whom they teased and hurt. In other words, I do not seek revenge or anything in that nature.

To conclude with a more *happier* section of this short story, I am not *always* sad over small hypotheticals. Being older, I learned to quickly shut off the sadness once it started to not regress back to when I was younger. However, it sometimes occurs to this day, and occasionally, it still troubles me.

Nevertheless, I have always employed a sense of humor. Since it is hard for me to forget things that I see, hear, or watch on television, I have retold and acted out jokes and funny monologues. I came up with a lot of my own as well. I always made the class smile and burst out laughing. I have actually gotten in trouble for using my sense of humor at the wrong time; sometimes, it was distracting for the class.

In third grade, when I was sort of the new kid at a new

school, I pretended to take expressions like "Take a hike" literally. I was mad that people did not want to play with me, being new and socially shy and all. On top of this, I had a hard-to-understand impediment. I did it for attention.

Plus, I could not stand estimation. When someone says something will happen at "2:30" for instance, I expect that it will not be at 2:29 or 2:31 but at precisely 2:30.

Soon, the teasing and sociable shyness dissipated as I started to make more and more friends.

Unsurprisingly, in June 2006, I was awarded by my fifth-grade teacher for the use of my sense of humor. I got the perfect attendance award too that year. Thus, I *always* made the class and my teacher laugh practically every school day.

It is a pleasure to make others feel great and laugh alongside my sense of humor. To cheer people up is my joy. One time at Ensign Intermediate, I walked out to my physical education class with a smile. One of my friends came up to me and said that he was feeling very down, but when he saw my smile, he felt better. He told me never to stop smiling.

That is the epitome of my main goal and what I strive for—to utilize my talents, smiles, and humor to make people happy. I always especially enjoyed putting smiles and joy on children's faces.

One of my first recollections of implementing slapstick comedy was in preschool, but it was unintentional. I had just gotten off the school bus and was walking toward my classroom at College Park Elementary. I saw my teachers and was waving, but suddenly, I nearly tripped over a tricycle. I could not believe that I missed it. I did not see it there. The teachers and I started laughing, and I pretended to do it again the next time and probably the time after that.

In first or second grade at Paularino Elementary, I went to

my desk to sit down. All of a sudden, I was on the floor. My chair was much farther back than I thought. My teacher and the class laughed with me. After that I pretended to do it a couple more times. The last time *was* the last time, though, for my teacher started to get mad at me for pretending.

In sixth grade at Newport Heights Elementary, I got to collect the attendance sheet from every classroom for a week. The far back portable was a fourth-grade class, and by midweek, when they saw me coming, they knew that I was going to make them all laugh. It was probably a Thursday or Friday when the finale happened. The fourth-grade teacher was by the door, and I was walking away backward, saying goodbye. Suddenly, I got this wild idea. I fell backward, dropping all the attendance sheets on the floor. The next thing I know, I heard incredibly loud stomps from the stampede of the entire class, rushing toward the door and window to see if I was okay. I could not resist.

Thankfully, I did not receive any repercussions, and we all laughed. I spent the next length of time on a bench organizing all of the attendance sheets scrupulously—being OCD and everything, I guess.

And there are a plethora of other examples.

In conclusion, the final, sad hypothetical that I once thought of before is that of a person who is disheartened due to a disability. Perchance they cannot read, write, see, walk, talk, hear, or speak like everybody else can. Maybe they are diabetic or are allergic to certain things.

And I am considered in that category of people who have a disability, along with an innumerable quantity of those who struggle with autism and Asperger's syndrome. For me, I know and trust that God has created me the way I am for His purpose. You now know how I did not let any of these hardships described in this anthology inundate me. I did not allow any of it to make me give up on my purpose in life, for Jesus has never given up on me.

I trust that I am fearfully and wonderfully made, as Psalm 139:34 tells me. Furthermore and importantly, God loves me and has a plan for my life. I have already started piecing His plan together, little by little, for He does not reveal everything at once. Otherwise, if we knew our calling, we would be lazy, assuming that it will happen one day without putting in the time, energy, and effort. I am excited to witness all of what He has planned for me and interchangeably, wherever *you* are at in life, He likewise loves you and has a plan for you.

About the Author

MATTHEW KENSLOW has grown up with a form of autism known as Asperger's Syndrome. Life has been an adventure as he pieced together all of his surroundings amid both praises and teases. His mission is to teach others from a firsthand perspective of how autistic people interpret things differently than the rest of the world.

He believes God has blessed him with the gifts to juggle, playing piano, and recalling facts about the American presidents, geography, science, and mathematics. He goes to juggle at elementary schools and encourages the children there to never give up on their passions.

He has earned the Gold Medal of Achievement (which is equivalent to the rank of Eagle Scout) through Royal Rangers, a program he has been in since he was five. Now, he is giving back to children and teenagers, teaching and mentoring them in a wide set of skills and knowledge.

He graduated Orange Coast College with an Associate of Science degree in Chemistry and is pursuing Vanguard University of Southern California. He currently aspires to be a middle school math and science teacher.

CPSIA information can be obtained
at www.ICGtesting.com
Printed in the USA
BVHW030948080822
644062BV00013B/194